TOWARD
LOVING

TOWARD *LOVING*

The Poetics of the Novel and the Practice of Henry Green

BY
BRUCE BASSOFF

UNIVERSITY OF SOUTH CAROLINA PRESS
COLUMBIA, S.C.

First Edition

Published by the University of South Carolina Press,
Columbia, S.C., 1975

Manufactured in the United States of America

Chapter II first appeared in abridged form as "Notes on the Language of Literature," pp. 65–73 in *Genre* 5 (March 1972) and is reprinted by permission of the publisher.

Chapter III first appeared in somewhat abridged form as "Prose Consciousness in the Novels of Henry Green," pp. 276–86 in *Language and Style* 5 (Fall 1972), and is reprinted by permission of the publisher.

Library of Congress Cataloging in Publication Data

Bassoff, Bruce, 1941–
Toward loving: the poetics of the novel and the practice of Henry Green.

Bibliography: p.
Includes index.
1. Green, Henry, 1905– —Criticism and interpretation. I. Title.
PR6013.R416Z58 823'.9'12 75-22071
ISBN 0–87249–324–5

To Allen Mandelbaum

CONTENTS

PREFACE

The original impulse behind this book was an interest in the novels of Henry Green. In the course of reading the few programmatic statements that Green has made about his novels and about the novel in general—statements regarding the nonrepresentational nature of fiction—it became clear to me that there were certain conceptual inadequacies in even the most serious treatments of Green and in discussions of the novel in general. I became concerned with two different sets of formal problems: those relating to the forms of life or to values; and those relating to the novel as a form, as a way of writing. In regard to the former, if we take the position of the earlier Georg Lukacs that the novel is characterized by a powerful ethical impulse, by a quest for authenticity, then we will have to confute the kind of neo-Arnoldian criticism that offers such standards as "the mainstream of life" and "traditional cultural forms." The extent to which the notion of a "great tradition" is progressive or reactionary depends on the extent to which it aids or hampers us in our efforts to identify the anthropological dimensions of literature. My own antagonism to the nouveau roman made me aware of the dangers of a consumer attitude toward values, sweetness and light being worth so much on the culture market.

The second set of formal problems has to do with the intrasystemic aspects of the novel, with the fact that novels signify as well as refer. The notion of verisimilitude is at best a banality and at worst a deception if it does not allow for the idea that language is an articulation of reality, a breaking up of what is undifferentiated, rather than a reflection of a reality which is ready-made. As we shall see, moreover, the conflict between writing and reality is as much a source of the novel's heuristic value as the mimesis assumed by the notion of verisimilitude.

As a result of these concerns, I intended to use Green's novels as a springboard for a discussion of some of the salient problems one faces in criticism of the novel. The organization of this study reflects that intention: an introductory chapter places Green in our literary and critical traditions; one chapter explores some of the parameters of novel criticism; and a sequence of chapters use Green's books to illustrate particular problems in analysis of the novel. By the time I had finished the penultimate chapter, however, it became apparent to me that in the course of trying to come to terms with certain problems in criticism of the novel, I had also been trying to come to terms with one particular novel by Henry Green—*Loving*. In other words, two opposite (though, hopefully, nonconflicting) movements were taking place in this study: an expansion in terms of the formal parameters that I found relevant to a discussion of the novel in general, and a contraction in terms of the particular test—*Loving*—toward which the book was moving.

Since I have not treated Green's novels in a systematic manner, a summary of each novel would have been awkward in the course of discussing some generic problem. Consequently, I have used an appendix to provide a novel-by-novel summary in order to eliminate problems of reference as we go along. These summaries will provide necessary background for readers who are unfamiliar with some or all of Green's novels and, it is hoped, will draw them to read those they have not. The page numbers that I have included in the text are from the following editions: *Back* (New York, 1950); *Blindness* (New York, 1926); *Caught* (New York, 1950); *Concluding* (New York, 1951); *Doting* (New York, 1952); *Living* (London, 1964); *Loving* (New York, 1949); *Nothing* (New York, 1950); *Pack My Bag* (London, 1952); *Party Going* (New York, 1951).

TOWARD
LOVING

I

Poetics and Practice

Bottom: Masters, you ought to consider with yourselves to bring in (God shield us!) a lion among ladies is a most dreadful thing. For there is not a more fearful wild-fowl than your lion living; and we ought to look to't.
Snout: Therefore another prologue must tell he is not a lion.
[*A Midsummer Night's Dream,* act 1 scene 1, 11.32–36]

HENRY GREEN is the pseudonym of Henry Vincent Yorke, Birmingham-London industrialist now retired. In the preface to an interview which Terry Southern conducted with Green are these autobiographical notes:

> I was born in 1905 in a large house by the banks of the river Severn, in England, and within the sound of the bells from the Abbey Church at Tewkesbury. Some children are sent away to school; I went at six and three-quarters and did not stop till I was twenty-two, by which time I was at Oxford, but the holidays were all fishing. And then there was billiards.
>
> I was sent at twelve and a half to Eton and almost at once became what was then called an aesthete, that is a boy who consciously dressed to shock. I stayed that way at Oxford. From Oxford I went into the family business, an engineering works in the Midlands, with its iron and brass foundries and machine shops. After working through from the bottom I eventually came to the top where for the time being I remain, married, living in London, with one son.[1]

The qualities that emerge from that interview, from his autobiography, and from John Russell's portrait of him, "There

[1] Terry Southern, "The Art of Fiction XXII, Henry Green," pp. 61–62.

It Is," are a combination of reticence and self-dramatization. Green has attempted insofar as possible to maintain his anonymity, pointing out to Southern the embarrassment his writing had caused him in his position as head of an industrial firm. In this interview, he uses his reputation for being hard of hearing to joke about some of the evaluative questions which Southern asks him, as when he mistakes "subtle" for "suttee."[2] Russell points out that Green fluctuates between extreme reservation and morbid exaggeration, both of which protect him from direct personal exposure and yet convey small bits of personal information indirectly.[3] It is noteworthy that Green uses his own deficiencies of health as thematic ploys and literary strategies in his books. His deafness appears most emphatically in *Concluding*, where old Mr. Rock keeps mistaking what people say to him and inadvertently making the kinds of verbal jokes which Green makes in his interview with Southern. That deafness is a model for the misunderstandings that pervade Green's books and provide much of their fabric. His diabetes and dyspepsia also appear as indices of a constitutional rejection of living—most frequently overcome by his characters.

At nineteen, while still a schoolboy at Eton, Green began his first novel, *Blindness*, which was to be published in 1926. The first section of the book is a diary of John Haye, a schoolboy whose attitudes and experiences at public school—including his aestheticism and his rebellion against the Officers Training Corps—resemble Green's own. The crisis that dislocates Haye's circumstances and forces him into a more immediate confrontation with life is his accidental blinding. The turning point in Green's own career was his decision, when the General Strike made him question his right to an inherited fortune, to leave Oxford in 1927 and enter life in a Birmingham factory. "It was," he said, "an introduction to indisputable facts at last, to a life bare of almost everything

[2] Ibid., pp. 64–65.
[3] John Russell, "There It Is," pp. 438–40.

except essentials and so less confusing, to a new world which was the oldest" (*Pack My Bag*, p. 236). Out of his experience as a factory worker came his second book, *Living*, in 1929, which deals with life in the factory and evinces a vigorous attentiveness to problems of prose style.

Green eventually became head of his family's industrial firm and remained a hardheaded businessman throughout his career as a writer. Even during his business career he was an omnivorous reader and did much of his writing during lunchtime at his office. Green's career was somewhat tangential to the careers of young intellectuals of the left (such as Auden and Isherwood) and to those of his more conservative contemporaries at Oxford (Waugh and Powell). In the thirties his position in the family's manufacturing firm steered him away from the world of letters, and in the forties he chose to enter the Fire Service, so he could keep a hand in his business (Waugh and Powell became army officers). Finally, Green moved permanently to London, whereas the other writers moved to the West Country.

In 1939 Green published his third novel, *Party Going*, which deals with an effete group of the Mayfair rich. In 1940 he published his autobiography, *Pack My Bag*, in which he described the prospect of war:

> One is always caught up, one inevitably has to take a hand but what I miss now is the reluctance I had then [at the time of the General Strike]. It is not that one was ever afraid to die. One may resent being killed, but most of us are quite ready. What is despairing in my case is that I should acquiesce, in the old days I should never have done so, and that is my farewell to youth in this absolute bewilderment of July 1939, that I should be so little unwilling to fight and yet likely enough to die by fighting for something which, as I am now, for the life of me I cannot understand.
>
> [Pp. 235–36.]

The war had an enormous and lasting effect on him, and out of this experience came his books of deep emotional trauma,

Caught (1943) and *Back* (1946). Green's position was that "except in disaster, life is oblique in its impact on people." Though the war provided one of those instances in which life's impact is most direct, in *Back* Green can get at the impact of this disaster only obliquely—by means of an erotic plot. In *Caught* the inadequate responses of the protagonist to the intense stress he suffers are supplemented by the author's more detailed evocations of this stress. Green's other novels are *Loving* (1945), *Concluding* (1948), *Nothing* (1950), and *Doting* (1952). By the time he had written his last two novels, Green seems to have developed a program for the English novel that emphasizes the reservations he had always had regarding epistemological certainty.

Indeed, Henry Green's novels do not fit comfortably into any of the major poetics of the novel that we have had in Anglo-American criticism: the Henry James–Percy Lubbock emphasis on point of view; the moral mimetic approach of F. R. Leavis and Irving Howe; or the apology for authorial intrusion of Wayne Booth. The first of these approaches is concerned with the problem of epistemological verisimilitude, which James qualifies as "intensity." After thinking out the situation and characters of such novels as *What Maisie Knew* and *The Ambassadors,* James discovered that intrigues could be more vital, more interesting, if the effort to solve them was incorporated into the book in the person of a central consciousness. That is, among the central character's other activities, his most interesting would be to guide our interests and perceptions by his own interests and perceptions. Opposing the omniscient point of view employed by Balzac, James claims that readers will not accept long stretches of retrospective analysis, that such illumination of motives should be dramatized in the action of the book itself. The James-Lubbock position is that we have access only to those experiences to which the central character has access, but that we supplement that character's perceptions with our own. In the case of *What Maisie Knew,* for example, we supplement

Maisie's inadequate formulation of her experiences with our own more sophisticated language. The "we," of course, is a collaboration of artist and reader. The moral-mimetic approach to fiction, on the other hand, is not concerned specifically with point of view or with showing versus telling, the other major concern of the James-Lubbock orientation. That is, its concerns are not primarily epistemological but moral and social. While F. R. Leavis's "great tradition" involves a notion of moral seriousness that has to do with the scope and quality of a writer's engagement with life, Irving Howe's essays in *Politics and the Novel* concern the novel's accurate reflection of socio-historical reality. For example, he rejects Joseph Conrad's use of "the secret agent" as a metaphor for the fragmentation of self in an urban environment and insists that Conrad should have created a more realistic picture of his terrorists. Finally, Wayne Booth's *The Rhetoric of Fiction* is a plea for flexibility in narrative method. Examining the epistemological concerns of James and Lubbock, Booth points out on the one hand that no author can really avoid intruding into his work in order to persuade his readers of some fact or value, and on the other hand that readers tend to concede certain privileges to an author that conflict with their sense of how we come to know things in real life. In his discussion of *Tristram Shandy,* moreover, he claims that telling can be a form of showing; that intrusions of a narrator (omniscient or otherwise) can have as realistic an effect as straight scenic presentation.[4]

Henry Green's critical terminus is closest to the Henry James of *The Awkward Age.* (In 1950 and 1951 Green made three public statements concerning the English novel, in which he advocated a novel made up entirely of dialogue, with a minimum of stage directions.) Green's epistemological wariness is significantly more pronounced, however, than that

[4] See Wayne Booth, *The Rhetoric of Fiction;* Irving Howe, *Politics and the Novel;* F. R. Leavis, *The Great Tradition;* and Percy Lubbock, *The Craft of Fiction.*

of James. If James sets himself certain limits in terms of the central consciousness that is recording events and undergoing bewilderment in his novels, it is only to dramatize those limits and compensate for them by deeper probings along the lines set by the central consciousness. The involuted syntax of James's later novels is in part an attempt to reconcile the limitations of his registering agents with the novelist's (and reader's) ambition for meaning. Whether the central consciousness of James's books is Strether or a little girl, his style is equally as deliberate and precise—as if the effort at understanding in the book has been underwritten by the narrator. One recalls, moreover, the "hideously intelligent" characters of *The Wings of the Dove,* who incorporate the language, the exposition of motives we normally associate with an omniscient narrator. Henry Green, for the most part, is uninterested in problems of point of view. The only novel in which a central consciousness plays a similar role to the dramatized observers in James's novels is *Back,* in which the protagonist is obsessively reenacting the trauma he has suffered during the war. Opposing the flexibility which Booth allows an author, however, Green insists that a respect for our epistemological limitations is essential to the creation of life in the novel. After pointing out that the imagination, in its silent communion with print, must be fired up, Green says:

> For a long time I thought this was best lit by very carefully arranged passages of description. But if I have come to hold as I do now, that we learn almost everything in life from what is done after a great deal of talk, then it follows that I am beginning to have my doubts about the uses of description. No; communication between the novelist and his reader will tend to be more and more by dialogue, until in a few years' time someone will think up something better.[5]

The two books Green wrote to fit his critical specifications, *Nothing* (1950) and *Doting* (1952), are failures by Green's

[5] Henry Green, "A Novelist to His Readers," p. 506.

own standard. *Nothing*, especially, contains lush descriptive passages that seem to have little function in the book except as verbal cadenzas. As such they contain a strong element of self-parody, as does the gratuitous detail in *Doting* that Peter is to bring a goose back to school. In contrast to *The Awkward Age*, where James writes a novel that approaches the condition of a play but is infinitely more complex than anything the theater could accommodate, Green's last two novels seem to parody the superficiality (in a nonpejorative sense) of Green's best novels. Despite the fact that Green's primary mode is scenic presentation, his best novels seem to entail a delicate balance between description and dialogue that is lacking in his programmatic novels.

The problem of mimetic responsibility is probably the most difficult in relation to Green and to the novel in general. Green says of representation in art:

> The colour used by painters in painting might seem to indicate that painters see more colour than do the general public. This, however, is doubtful. It is extraordinary the number of professional painters there are with poor eyesight. It is more likely that as they become expert at their art they get involved in the tones and composition of their picture while they are painting, one tone or shade of colour leading to another until this evolves into a harmonious whole which may have little direct relation to nature. Thereby painters produce something which isn't, that is to say, the result is non-representational, and yet if and when the painting is successful, it has a life of its own.
>
> This is also true of a good novel.[6]

This kind of critical statement is rather surprising in so mimetic a critical climate. It sounds much more like the statements which many contemporary French critics and novelists have been making about fiction. It is interesting to note in this respect that Nathalie Sarraute talks about Green in her essay on "conversation and sub-conversation" as a practitioner

[6] Green, "The English Novel of the Future," p. 21.

of a "new novel" relying on words rather than acts to stimulate the imagination of the reader.[7] The French nouveau roman has developed side by side with a body of criticism loosely called structuralist ("loosely" in the sense that some of its practitioners reject the appellation). If Green was a novelist writing without the critics at hand who had the poetic to fit him, the nouveau romanists are in an especially privileged situation, where practice and poetics move abreast. In fact, Gérard Genette sees contemporary literature as taking over the traditional function of rhetoric, since it is both literature and discourse on literature; Roland Barthes sees no essential difference in technique between structuralist criticism on the one hand and literature on the other. The structuring activity is the same whether the primary object is found in the "social real" or the "imaginary real," whether the result is an essay or a novel.[8]

The primary targets of the structuralist critique are the traditional notion of mimesis and the ideological character of the traditional or bourgeois novel, which, with its accompanying notions of character, story, form and content, and social responsibility, is considered outmoded. Roland Barthes points out that while the bourgeoisie built its power on its scientific and technological transformations of nature, its ideology restores an inalterable nature; while its own status is historical, its ideology charges that status with universality. That is, if the historical achievements of the bourgeoisie represent a kind of anti-nature, its ideology replaces that antinature with a kind of pseudo-nature.[9] In the traditional novel, narrative signs like the preterit and the third person singular suggest a logical order underlying the universe. Not only does the interior furniture of Balzac's world furnish clear indices of value (quantity and price representing the differences be-

[7] Nathalie Sarraute, *The Age of Suspicion*, pp. 51–75.

[8] See Roland Barthes, *Critical Essays*, p. 215; and Gérard Genette, *Figures II*, p. 41.

[9] Barthes, *Mythologies*, pp. 141–42.

tween men) but nature itself is humanized. Mountains and rivers exist not merely in themselves but also to illustrate human characteristics of nobility, fickleness, and the like. The story in the traditional novel is univocal, innocent, governed by immutable laws of cause and effect. Its verisimilitude is achieved by motivation since it has lost the transparency of older forms of narrative, which relied on commonplaces about human behavior and on actions deemed suitable to a genre in order to gain the acceptance of their audience. The bourgeois novel seeks to gain the transparency of older forms by multiplying explanations, by providing ad hoc commonplaces or maxims of human behavior.[10] Opposing the traditional novel's reinforcement of bourgeois ideology, its naturalization of culture, Barthes proposes a literature that annuls the accretions of sense, the myths that delimit our perceptions. The technique of literature must suspend this sense and, in its ambiguity and reticence, maintain a questioning of the world. Barthes's analysis of Robbe-Grillet's novels points to the destruction of sense which the novelist accomplishes in his flat descriptions, superficial anecdotes, and insecure personages; to the kind of interrogation or astonishment that his novels achieve despite his theoretical error in supposing that there is an object "out there" that is not subject to man's significations and that is then the object of a greater realism in the novel. Nature, according to Barthes, is always signifying; if literature can perform the function of designification, it is an admirable artifice responding to a cultural need. Content always slips back into these emptied forms, but literature is a constant purging of this plethora of sense, a silence in the midst of the continuous chatter that surrounds us. Of the statue pointing uncertainly in the garden of *Last Year at Marienbad,* Barthes says, "Perhaps all literature is in this anaphoric suspension which at one and the same time desig-

[10] See Barthes, *Writing Degree Zero,* pp. 29–40; and Genette, *Figures II,* pp. 71–99.

nates and keeps silent."[11] Although he does not acknowledge the connection, Barthes's notion of a literature that signifies without ever yielding a sense is much like Kant's criterion for the aesthetic idea—purposiveness without purpose. The aesthetic object stimulates a purposive activity that exercises the understanding or the moral faculty without ever yielding a concept, a sense of closure. Whereas Kant turns to nature for some reassurance that the purposes of man can be effected, that the purposiveness of art is answered by a purposiveness of nature, Barthes is satisfied with the tautological status of art, its complete lack of transitivity.

The problem of mimesis and of the language of fiction is as difficult as that of ideology. We seem to have little difficulty in recognizing that the formal parameters of verse (*découpage* or line ending, meter, rhyme) provide it with certain internal laws that have nothing to do with verisimilitude. We seem often to talk about the novel, however, as imitation, almost as if the text could be taken for an external reality to which it refers, like an impersonator being taken for the object of his impersonation. Christopher Caudwell, for example, states that "rhythm, 'preciousness' and style are alien to the novel [for] novels are not composed of words. They are composed of scenes, actions, stuff, and people, just as plays are. A 'jewelled' style is a disadvantage to a novel because it distracts the eye from the things and people to the words—not as words, as black outlines, but as symbols to which a variety of feeling-tone is attached."[12] Aristotle's notion of diction seems to be an embarrassment in this account of the novel, as is the distinction between narrative and scene, two different modes of presentation.[13] Caudwell wishes to minimize the mediation of experience by language, the hetero-

[11] Barthes, *Critical Essays,* pp. 203–4.

[12] Christopher Caudwell, *Illusion and Reality,* p. 200.

[13] Note that Else, in his formidable analysis of the *Poetics,* evades the problems of lexical deviation raised in Chapter 22. See Gerald F. Else, *Aristotle's Poetics,* pp. 567–68.

geneity between the signifier and the thing signified: "The poetic Word is the Logos, the word-made-flesh, the active will ideally ordering; whereas the novel's word is the symbol, the reference, the conversationally pointing gesture."[14]

It is against this notion of fiction as a sign whose adequacy we can judge by the efficiency, the painlessness, with which it refers us to an external reality that critics like Barthes are rebelling. Just as Gilbert Ryle distinguishes between "knowing how" and "knowing that" in *The Concept of Mind,* these critics want to distinguish between a prose that is ministering to a set purpose (convincing people that a surtax is necessary, for example) and a prose that is in process, that is discovering itself as it goes along. They are not talking about automatic writing but writing generated by laws peculiar to literary activity rather than laws peculiar to economics, ethics, or politics. In verse this point is easy to see: the content of a poem is determined in great part by the formal tasks a poet assumes—to realize a given verse form such as a sonnet or a villanelle or a less traditional prosodic scheme. At the very least, verse entails line endings which provide formal resistance to the unfolding of the proposition. The conventions of the novel are much less conspicuous, since, except for the chapter, they do not provide the resistance to natural discourse (as we see it, for example, in the anecdote) that the formal parameters of verse provide.

Verisimilitude in the traditional novel has been achieved primarily by psychological motivation and by the circumstantial particularity of details. Whereas the former tends to disguise the fact that events in a narrative have the function of making possible other events in the narrative, the latter tends to disguise the fact that the novel is not analogous to real life. For example, description in the novel does not really reproduce perception. In the first place, one can never exhaust verbally the elements of a scene or the qualities of

[14] Caudwell, p. 247.

an object perceived in real life. In the second place, whereas in real life we perceive simultaneously a multitude of objects or the qualities of one object, we perceive the descriptive elements of fiction one after another. Ironically, the more exhaustive an author tries to be in his descriptions, the more unrealistic they are, since the reader's verbal memory is limited: No sooner does he assimilate a new detail than he loses his hold on details which have preceded it. The more elaborately the description unfolds, the more completely the scene dissolves. Writers of the nouveau roman like Jean Ricardou and Alain Robbe-Grillet play on this phenomenon to stress the autonomy of writing and the conventional nature of our perceptions. Sometimes description functions almost entirely on a rhetorical level—that is, at the same time that its exhaustive quality frustrates our ability to visualize, the long series acts as a sign for the *vraisemblable*. One conspicuous example of this function is the enumeration we get in *Moll Flanders:* "And I went thro' into *Bartholomew Close,* and then turn'd round to another passage that goes into *Long lane,* so away into *Charterhouse-Yard* and out into *St. John's street,* then, crossing into *Smithfield,* went down Chick Lane and into Field Lane to *Holbornbridge*. . . ."[15] The eye skims over the passage and registers it as signifying Fact. One also notes the verbal unreality characterizing the work of Helen Keller, whose journals contain elaborate descriptions of nature, down to the drop of dew glistening in the sunlight (which obviously signified nature to her but which bore no reference).

Another problem concerning the relation between fiction and real life is the assimilation in fiction of the real and the virtual (meaning by "virtual" dreams, hallucinations, etc.). In Ambrose Bierce's "An Occurrence at Owl Creek Bridge," a man condemned to hang is described as attempting to es-

[15] Daniel Defoe, *Moll Flanders,* ed. J. Paul Hunter, pp. 153–54. All quotations are from this edition.

cape his captors after the rope has broken. In a passage of breathless action, Bierce writes:

Suddenly he heard a sharp report and something struck the water smartly within a few inches of his head, spattering his face with spray. He heard a second report, and saw one of the sentinels with his rifle at his shoulder, a light cloud of blue smoke rising from the muzzle. The man in the water saw the eye of the man on the bridge gazing into his own through the sights of the rifle. He observed that it was a gray eye and remembered having read that gray eyes were keenest, and that all famous marksmen had them. Nevertheless, this one had missed.[16]

The force of the story depends on our accepting the premise that the rope has broken and that the victim is attempting to escape. At the end of the story, when the point of view shifts and we discover that these incidents were fantasies taking place instantaneously in the mind of the hanged man, we go back to passages like this one and realize their impossibility. How could a man in the water see the eye of a sentinel on a bridge through the sight of the latter's rifle? How could he know what color the man's eye was? Bierce's style is homogeneous, whether it is describing what we retrospectively classify as real or what we retrospectively classify as virtual. In *The Fantastic: A Structural Approach to a Literary Genre,* Tzvetan Todorov sees the supernatural as the "proof and consequence" of language. Since language enables us to conceive of what is not there, the devil and vampires have the same ontological status as the rhetorical figure. They are neither true nor false but modes of querying our perceptions of the world and our designs on each other. As a matter of fact, the supernatural is frequently born from our taking a figurative sense literally. For example, in Mérimée's *La Vénus d'Ille* a statue comes to life and strangles a man who has had the impudence to leave his wedding ring on her

[16] Ambrose Bierce, "An Occurrence at Owl Creek Bridge," pp. 38–39.

finger. Supernatural events in this story are preceded by rhetorical evocations of their possibility. For example, after one of the peasants says that the statue looks *as if* it is staring at one, this banality is realized by the animation of the statue. The protagonist refuses to send someone to get his wedding ring because people would be taken aback by his distraction. They would *call* him the husband of the statue. In fact the statue subsequently acts as if it were the hero's wife.[17] As we shall see, the literature of the fantastic is simply an exemplary mode of the unreality of language that all fiction discloses.

Gerald Else translates a passage from Chapter Four of Aristotle's *Poetics:* "For the reason they take pleasure in seeing the images is that in the process of viewing they find themselves learning, that is, reckoning what kind a given thing belongs to: 'This individual is a So-and-so.'" In a note to this passage Else, attempting to reconcile Aristotle's notion of the artist as imitator with his notion of the artist as maker, defines mimesis as species identification: "The connecting of the individual with the species is the crux of the matter."[18] Aristotle distinguishes between poetry and history by saying that the poet has to describe not what *has* happened but what *might* happen—that is, what is possible as being probable or necessary. Poetry, then, is more philosophic than history in that it deals with universals rather than particulars.

In seventeenth-century French fiction the same standard of verisimilitude applies. The confession of Madame de Clèves, for example, scandalized some critics who felt that the confession was so improbable it could only happen in a *real* story. The English novel, on the other hand, manifests in its beginnings a concern with the particularities of experience. Moll Flanders says of her reactions to her incestuous marriage, "I cannot say that I was right in point of policy in carrying it to such a length while at the same time I did not resolve to discover the thing to him; but I am giving an account of what

[17] Tzvetan Todorov, *The Fantastic,* pp. 75–90.
[18] Aristotle, *Poetics,* pp. 20, 85.

was, not of what ought or ought not to be" (p. 81). *Moll Flanders,* however, raises its own problems regarding mimesis, for the particularities of experience it "records" are of a special kind. Moll says of her first marriage, ". . . as he had not received much from them and had in the little time he lived acquired no great Matters, so my Circumstances were not great, nor was I much mended by the Match" (p. 49). Moll's vocabulary is abstract, locating particulars in their quantitative, not their qualitative, aspects. That is, mimesis is always a function, not only of the object, but also of the subject. In fact, subject and object are not always distinguishable, since the object of mimesis is frequently the knowing or desiring process of the subject. One could argue that what Defoe is imitating is the process by which a capitalist society converts use value into exchange value, the qualitative aspects of objects and people into their worth on the market. Point of view later becomes very important in bridging subject and object.

Let us assume for a moment that we know what we mean when we posit some sort of analogous relationship between the novel and real life. Going back to Else's notion of species identification, we may say that greater or lesser formal realism is a function of the degree to which members of a class of persons, events, or settings within a novel deviate from members of the same class of persons, events, or settings in real life or in culturally assimilated novels. We are immediately in difficulty, however, because the boundaries between these contiguous notions are constantly shifting. In her famous essay, "Mr. Bennett and Mrs. Brown," Virginia Woolf points out that for novelists like Galsworthy, Wells, and Bennett, character is a function of material circumstances, virtually inseparable from milieu. Woolf seems to be saying that literature has a life of its own, with conventions that enable the author and the reader to communicate. In this sense the conventions of the Edwardian novel are as good as the conventions of the "new novel," and it is only when they become shopworn that they lose their usefulness. At the same time, Woolf also claims that none of the Edwardian novelists were ever able to convey anything about human nature. Arnold Bennett might describe admirably every detail of the railway carriage in which Mrs. Brown sits, but he could never capture the elusive human quality of Mrs. Brown. The attempts of the Georgian novelists (Forster, Lawrence, Joyce) to convey this quality would cause a temporary debacle of communication in literature but would eventually generate new conventions.[19] The same dual standards appear in Nathalie Sarraute's more recent essay "The Age of Suspicion," where Sarraute debunks Woolf's contention that the primary responsibility of the novelist is to create real characters. Like Woolf, Sarraute on the one hand implies that all conventions are equal: Those of Balzac, having enabled him to convey the intensity of life, are as valid as the conventions of Joyce and Faulkner. One might add that our agreement to allow Faulkner's or Joyce's interior monologues to signify the inner life of the twentieth century is as arbitrary as the agreement of the nineteenth-century reader to allow Balzac's psychological expositions to signify the inner life of that time. On the other hand, Sarraute claims that changing conventions in the novel reflect our changing understanding of human reality. The "new novel" in Sarraute's critical writings (as in those of Robbe-Grillet) is associated with a "new reality." Writing about mimesis Sarraute claims that the same process is taking place in the novel that took place in painting: "The psychological element, like the pictorial element, is beginning to free itself imperceptibly from the object of which it was an integral part. . . . Since what the characters gain in the way of facile vitality and plausibility is balanced by a loss of fundamental truth in the psychological states for which they serve as props, he [the reader] must be kept from allowing his attention to wander or to be absorbed by

[19] Virginia Woolf, "Mr. Bennett and Mrs. Brown."

the characters."[20] The point about Nathalie Sarraute's sub-conversation (which has been adapted to the English novel by Christine Brooke-Rose) is that the subject becomes his own object, the separation between fiction and discourse being nullified. If traditional notions of mimesis posited a gap between the signifier and the thing signified, in Sarraute one has a totally homogeneous situation: The word is itself.

Writers as diverse as René Girard, Lucien Goldmann, and Roland Barthes want to redefine our conventional notion of mimesis. In his study *Deceit, Desire, and the Novel,* which ends with an apology for traditional Christian transcendence, Girard poses the question whether Proust's long novel has any sociological value. Assuming the realistic *qua* positivistic premises of the traditional novel, the answer is no. Proust does not draw up an inventory of political and social facts defining a given milieu; his work lacks the elaborate documentation of circumstances characterizing novelistic inquiries before him. A sociologist seeking to understand the properties of the Faubourg Saint-Germain would find the object of his research constantly eluding him. Unlike the sociologist, the novelist is not tyrannized by the object. His concern is not the object "as it is" or as it is transformed by desire but the process of transformation itself. Just as Cervantes is intrigued by the fact that Don Quixote confuses a barber's basin with Mambrino's helmet, Proust is struck by the fact that snobs can transform the Faubourg Saint-Germain into the kingdom of heaven:

> The sociologist and the naturalistic novelist want only one truth. They impose this truth on all perceiving subjects. What they call object is an insipid compromise between the incompatible perceptions of desire and nondesire. This object's credibility comes from its intermediate position, which weakens all the contradictions. Instead of taking the edge off these contradictions the great novelist sharpens them as much as possible. He underscores the meta-

[20] Sarraute, *The Age of Suspicion,* pp. 68–69.

morphoses brought about by desire. The naturalistic writer does not perceive this metamorphosis because he is incapable of criticizing his own desire. The novelist who reveals triangular desire cannot be a snob but he must have been one. He must have known desire but must now be beyond it.[21]

Discussing the collective character of literary creation, the Marxist critic Lucien Goldmann claims that the structures of literary works are homologous to the mental structures of certain groups or are in an intelligible relationship with them, whereas their contents, the imaginary universes ruled by these structures, are freely chosen by the writer. It is in this sense, Goldmann claims, that Nathalie Sarraute and Robbe-Grillet are two of the most radically realistic writers in contemporary French literature.[22] Roland Barthes also disclaims the positivist approach toward fiction, especially its attempts to find the genesis of certain elements of a work in corresponding elements of reality. Mimesis entails not an analogy of substances but an analogy of functions (what Lévi-Strauss calls homology). Barthes departs from Goldmann in that he does not feel that the structure of a work of art is homologous to the mental structure of a certain social class. The artist's imagination can distort or pervert his social situation as well as reproduce it. The whole of the work is homologous to the whole of the author.[23]

This critique of positivism, especially as it relates to the traditional novel, echoes Henry Green's distinction between the novelist and the journalist: The journalist presents as straightforward an account as he can of the events he is reporting, the novelist tries to stimulate the reader's imagination; the journalist presents the most expedient explanation of phenomena, the novelist attempts to keep the reader questioning.

[21] René Girard, *Deceit, Desire, and the Novel,* pp. 216–20.
[22] Lucien Goldmann, *Pour une sociologie du roman,* pp. 281–324.
[23] Barthes, *Critical Essays,* pp. 251–53.

Accordingly, the journalist's approach must be the most direct of which he is capable, and the novelist's approach must be oblique. In life the intimations of reality are nearly always oblique. In other words, you learn more from the lies of someone who is speaking to you, if you can find these out, than you will from direct statements which generally only represent a portion of what the person you are speaking to believes. A direct lie can be infinitely revealing, and a half-truth when heard gets us nowhere. Accordingly, the treatment of dialogue by the novelist will be oblique, that is to say, there should be no direct answers in dialogue. If the fictional characters A and B are talking together in narrative, A should ask a question on which B should ask another, although the natural fatigue of the reader over such inconclusiveness should be carefully watched for.[24]

It is thus the obliqueness of human experience that Green is trying to recreate in his fiction, whether the obliqueness has to do with our awareness of the world or with our awareness of our own desire (the two, as René Girard points out, are ultimately one). Green's epistemological position reminds one of Mario Untersteiner's citation of Gorgias: "'Tragedy,' he says, 'with its myths and its emotions has created a deception such that its successful practitioner is nearer to reality than the unsuccessful, and the man who lets himself be deceived is wiser than he who does not.'"[25] In this manner one arrives at the irremediable contradiction of existence.

Green's critical reception has generally been favorable, although some critics have disputed the suitability of some of his literary experimentation to a priori commitments that they assign him as a novelist. At one end of this critical spectrum is Robert Phelps, who states: "The writer in whose work there exists something like a true marriage between vision and medium, is, today, so much the exception that in reckoning with him—with a poet like Robert Graves, or a

[24] Green, "The English Novel of the Future," p. 25. In this connection, note Girard's *mensonges romantiques* and his disparagement of the "compromise" of naturalistic fiction.

[25] Mario Untersteiner, *The Sophists,* pp. 113–14.

novelist like Henry Green—we have to acknowledge a difference in kind. He is more, perhaps, like a composer. His works are more organic. They can be distinguished from, but never profitably compared to, those of less 'married writers.' "[26] Philip Toynbee's view of Green's achievement is similar, if somewhat qualified. Conceding that Green chose to take risks with his prose in order to convey a new vision, Toynbee complains that this vision lacks "compassion," that Green's works lack a real "moral effect," as contrasted with the works of E. M. Forster.[27] At the other end of the spectrum is Orville Prescott, who sees Green as a coterie writer whose attitudes toward life and literary form are unhealthy. Instead of interpreting the "main stream of life," Green's novels express a sense of victimization by the chaos of modern life. Instead of maintaining a continuity with "traditional cultural forms," Green indulges in effete experimentation that becomes an end in itself.[28] This view of fiction has been reiterated in George Steiner's recent apology for C. P. Snow, where he contrasts "daylight" writers like Snow (interested in political, social, and economic "truths") with writers who are concerned with "the dynamics of feeling and language."[29] Similar criticism was leveled at Tennyson and other Victorian writers for not dealing with matters of public importance and not expounding the necessary public optimism in their work. It is noteworthy that in Victorian literature poetry represents a sort of underground for socially disapproved feelings, where the scholar-gypsy, among others, took refuge.

In the twentieth century the novel has become one of the forums in which our humanistic assumptions have been challenged. Although this challenge has taken its most radical form in the nouveau roman, where several "obsolete notions" have been challenged by Robbe-Grillet, Sarraute, and others, David

[26] Robert Phelps, "The Vision of Henry Green," p. 614.
[27] Philip Toynbee, "The Novels of Henry Green," pp. 490–95.
[28] Orville Prescott, *In My Opinion*, pp. 104–5.
[29] George Steiner, "Last Stop for Mrs. Brown," p. 84.

Daiches observes a similar challenge in modern English fiction:

> The older English novelist selected what were the significant things in the behavior of his characters on a principle publicly shared, and part of that publicly shared principle was the fact that what was significant in human events was itself manifested in publicly visible doing or suffering, in action or passion related to status or fortune. The modern novelist is born when that publicly shared principle of selection and significance is no longer felt to exist, can no longer be depended on. The reasons for this breakdown of the public background of belief are related to new ideas in ethics, psychology, and many other matters as well as to social and economic factors.[30]

When Toynbee misses the moral seriousness of Forster in Green's books, what he is really looking for is the residue of the central, moral consciousness that we find in *Tom Jones,* which controls our responses to the book. In *Howards End,* which Lionel Trilling considers Forster's best novel, we have such a central consciousness not only controlling our reading of the book but invading the consciousness of the book's characters. The utterances or thoughts of these characters, then, become clearly programmatic. At one point Helen Schlegel thinks, "Death destroys a man: the idea of Death saves him." At another point Forster remarks in his own voice, "Death destroys a man, but the idea of death saves him—that is the best account of it that has yet been given." Similarly, Margaret Schlegel remarks at one point: "Had you thought it, then? That there are two kinds of people—our kind who live straight from the middle of their heads, and the other kind who can't, because their heads have no middle? They can't say 'I.' " Forster later writes: "As he [Charles] watched his father shuffling up the road, he had a vague regret—a wish that something had been different somewhere—a wish (though he did not express it thus) that he had been taught to say

[30] David Daiches, *The Novel and the Modern World,* pp. 4–5.

'I' in his youth." Forster's frequent lapses into the tendentious are one of the liabilities of his confident relationship with his audience. Similar lapses pervade D. H. Lawrence's books, where scenes merely demonstrate Lawrence's ideas instead of realizing the tensions that underlie those ideas. Contrast the scene in which Gerald Crich invades Gudrun's bedroom, tracking the dirt of the graveyard in with him—a scene that powerfully realizes the love-as-death characterizing their relationship—with the scene in which Ursula intrudes on Birkin's throwing stones at the reflection of the moon. He cries, "Cybele—curse her! The accursed Syria Dea! Does one begrudge it her? What else is there—?" Ursula and Birkin then engage in a long, labored discussion of the meaning of his action. The tendentiousness in Lawrence, however, stems from another cause than Forster's. Whereas the assumption underlying Forster's voice is a cultural homogeneity (like that assumed by Fielding), which makes for a confident relationship between Forster and his public, the assumption underlying Lawrence's voice is cultural discontinuity and heterogeneity, brought about by industrial civilization. Two kinds of dangers beset a novel invested with the kind of prophetic impulse that characterizes Lawrence's novels. On the one hand, the novel can become allegory, in the sense that the drive to translate the life of the novel into certain ideas may vitiate that life. Birkin's throwing stones at the reflection of the moon is an example of this kind of translatability. On the other hand, the novel can collapse into essay, which happens often in Birkin's extended disquisitions. At his best, however, in parts of *The Rainbow* and *Women in Love*, Lawrence is able to evoke the burdens of consciousness entailed by cultural change.

The greater moral value that Toynbee finds in Forster has to do with the a priori moral concerns investing his books—concerns that have basically to do with the limitations of class and the power of tradition. Similar to the problems posed by the echo in *Passage to India*, the questions asked by Forster seem important. Such a priori concerns are not as conspicuous in Green's work, which eschews the kind of discursiveness we have noted in Forster. Green, as opposed to Wayne Booth, believes that at one time perhaps novels could be given life by means of authorial comment, but that this is no longer true. In contrast with Forster's constant overview of his story and with his use of melodramatic plot constructions to generate significant conflicts, Green states: "For how do we, each one of us, find out anything in the lives we each lead? Very little by reading, still less by what we are told. We get experience, which is as much knowledge as we shall ever have, by watching the way people around us behave, after they have spoken."[31] Russell notes that in March 1926, while Green was traveling on the Continent, he wrote notes to himself contrasting his use of experience with his use of books. Despite his omnivorous reading, despite the value that the schoolboy diarist in *Blindness* places on books ("What a force books are!"), Green seemed to feel that a general recollection of books is what he should achieve: "He seemed to be cautioning himself about getting too bound up in artifacts. After he had drawn up a list of ways to remember, 'Remembering by quotation' drew disparagement from him; as for experience . . . he had put down on his list the phrase 'Remembering by the significant irrelevance.' "[32] This phrase would seem to place him in the spectrum of twentieth-century English fiction—away from the role of the cultural ombudsman and in the area of epiphany represented by Joyce's *Dubliners* and Woolf's *To the Lighthouse*. This area involves a democratization of human concerns, a sense that the richness of life can best be disclosed in the random moment. The rhetoric of clear and distinct ideas (the motivation of Balzac's characters or the sentimental education of Forster's) gives way to a rhetoric of ambiguity (Bloom's homecoming, Mr. Ramsay's arrival at the lighthouse).

[31] Green, "A Novelist to His Readers," p. 506.
[32] Russell, "There It Is," p. 444.

II

Commonplaces

Pas une seule fois un de mes personnages ne ferme une fenêtre, ne se lave les mains, ne passe un pardessus, ne dit une formule de présentation. S'il y avait même quelque chose de nouveau dans ce livre, ce serait cela. . . ."

[Marcel Proust to Robert Dreyfus, 29 November 1913, in *Correspondance Générale,* vol. 4 (Paris: Librairie Plon, 1933), p. 260.]

Marxist critic Lucien Goldmann claims that it is no accident that structuralism and the nouveau roman, both of which are characterized by an absence of subject (in the linguistic sense) and a disparagement of history, occur at the same time. His explanation is that our growing alienation—our sense that objects are becoming more and more autonomous and men more and more like objects—accounts for the rise of a nongenetic structuralism. The ultimate ambition for critics Barthes and Tzvetan Todorov is to find in literature an equivalent of the "science of myths" that they attribute to Lévi-Strauss. For Lévi-Strauss, the mind operates among a sequence of choices posed by binary alternatives—such as the cooked and the raw, the high and the low, the changed and the unchanged—which are the primary material of man's imagination. Just as generative grammar attempts to analyze sentences in terms of rules of transformation that the speaker applies to certain grammatical modules, structural mythology attempts to show that all cultural phenomena are transformations of certain basic structures. Going beyond the sentence to the logic of symbolic (literary) discourse, Barthes and Todorov want to show that all literary works involve transformation of basic themes. Just as we can judge the grammaticalness of a sentence by our linguistic competence, so can we judge the acceptability of certain themes in certain contexts by our competence in signification. For example, in his study of the fantastic Todorov discusses two kinds of themes: those of "I" or of perception and those of "you" or of discourse. Whereas the first involves a breaking down of the barriers between self and world, mental and material, words and objects, the second involves a breaking out of the libido, a transgression of social restraint. This transgression can be simply verbal (the word becoming equivalent to the act), since language is the structuring agent in the relations between men. Balzac's *Louis Lambert* scandalizes us because these two incompatible themes are included in the same work.[1] The obverse of these epistemological claims is an emphasis on the internal relations of literary elements, their ability to enter into correlation with one another, rather than their reference to social or psychological phenomena outside the work. For example, one can make judgments about the relation between two textual elements (the puppet Olimpia and the childhood of Nathaniel in E. T. A. Hoffmann's *The Man of Sand*), but one cannot make judgments about the relations between Hoffmann's work and his own childhood. This emphasis on the function of an element rather than on its genesis is part of a general strategy of seeing the whole work as determined by structural or spatial relationships rather than by causal or genetic ones.

Lucien Goldmann thinks that this nongenetic structuralism is insufficient because it does not enable us to know whether we have discerned in a work a structure that is pertinent to its meaning. His critique of critics like Barthes is similar to the critique that Michael Riffaterre makes of Jakobson and Lévi-Strauss's approach to Baudelaire's "Les Chats." Riffaterre claims that Jakobson and Lévi-Strauss multiply linguistic structures without convincing us that they are all pertinent to a reading of the poem.[2] Goldmann believes that our positing a structure in a work of art must be controlled by locating a more global structure that explains the work. To account for the structure of Racine's tragedies of refusal, and to ex-

[1] Tzvetan Todorov, *The Fantastic,* pp. 107–39.
[2] Michael Riffaterre, "Describing Poetic Structures," pp. 200–42.

plain their similarity to Pascal's *Pensées*, one first has to derive the figures of God, Man, and the World from the particular characters of those plays and then to insert that configuration into the world view of extremist Jansenism. Goldmann's notion of function, unlike the intrasystemic notion of the structuralists, is the way in which a work of art realizes imaginatively the vision of the world implicit in a given social class. That vision, in turn, is a complex response to the class's socio-historical circumstances. Whereas Barthes sees Robbe-Grillet's novels as exemplifying the periodic purging or designation of language that takes place in modern fiction, Goldmann sees Robbe-Grillet's novels as homologous in form to the reification characteristic of a highly advanced stage of capitalism, where the boundaries between men and things have broken down. If Barthes is concerned primarily with how a literary work signifies rather than with what it signifies (almost always an ideology that makes an abusive use of language), Goldmann shares Georg Lukacs's view that ideologies are our way of organizing experience and should be judged by how much of the whole of society they enable us to understand. If, for Barthes, classical literature suffers from a nauseating integument of social and psychological commonplaces, and if modern literature has a demythologizing function, for Goldmann all great literature, whether classical or modern, reflects the major socio-historical contradictions of its period.[3]

If we consider the following adumbration of the field of critical activity,

life
(*praxis*)

values
(form)
(interpretation)

art
(form)
(description)

[3] See Roland Barthes, *S/Z*, pp. 210–12, and Lucien Goldmann, *Pour une sociologie du roman*, pp. 281–324, 337–63.

we note two kinds of formalism: that of structuralist critics and writers of the nouveau roman, who restrict their critical activity to the *level* of artistic form, to the correlations of elements within a work; and that of the earlier Georg Lukacs, who is concerned with the problem of how we can make life essential, of how we can realize values that make sense of duration. Both kinds of formalists wage a polemic against time: Lukacs because time is a destroyer of values, Robbe-Grillet and Barthes because time implies the power of history. For Lukacs a realm of *praxis* lies behind and is antecedent to language; that *praxis* is more important than the words one is writing. For Robbe-Grillet and Barthes literature is no longer subsumed under the notion of mimesis. The novelist asks his reader "no longer to receive ready-made a world completed, full, closed upon itself, but on the contrary to participate in a creation, to invent in his turn the work—and the world—and thus to learn to invent his own life."[4] The word is primary, and no realm of *praxis* is prior to the activity of the novelist. Jean Ricardou, another critic and nouveau romanist, deals with problems relating to the time of reading and the time of the fiction, but he does not deal with time as plenitude or deprivation, with time as completing something.

In order to put these problems in perspective, let us consider Georg Lukacs's *The Theory of the Novel.* Lukacs places the novel between the epic and the tragedy. In the former there is congruence—in the latter there is an unbridgeable gap—between self and the world, between the empirical and the intelligible. In the closed society of epic, neither the individual nor the world is problematic: The individual is a function of a limited number of roles (priest, king, warrior) and his differentiation from other men is only in terms of his competence to fulfill those roles, one symptom of which is his relationships with the gods. The participating gods of epic ensure that the action is intelligible. Despite the capricious-

[4] Alain Robbe-Grillet, *For a New Novel,* p. 156.

ness of the gods, the epic hero is at home in the world and is always adequate to his fate. On the other hand, despite the rationalization of hubris, the tragic hero is alienated from the world and from his fate; his situation is a metaphor for the arbitrariness of death. The gods of tragedy are inscrutable, hypermetropic. In the novel, the forms of life are not immanent, as they are in the epic; but, unlike the tragedy, the novel attempts to bridge the gap between self and world, the empirical and the intelligible, by means of reflection. Philosophy is both a symptom of that hiatus and the hope for bridging it.[5] The world of epic is timeless (as Auerbach points out, there is no sliding perspective in Homer; even events in the past are foregrounded in an absolute present).[6] In the novel the hiatus between inner and outer gives birth to a sense of time which is the destroyer of values (in Flaubert's *Sentimental Education*, time becomes the trace of disillusionment). Concomitantly, however, memory becomes a means of redemption, a possible mode of reuniting the inner and the outer.[7] The novel also makes possible prophecy or apocalypse, a mode which Lukacs (and E. M. Forster also) talks about in connection with Dostoevski.[8] The nouveau roman, like the epic, is a mode of absolute presentness. Robbe-Grillet uses agrammatical syntax in *The Voyeur* in order to bring into the foreground of absolute presentness events taking place at different moments in time. Whereas the epic is timeless because the forms of life are immanent, the nouveau roman is timeless because it has cut its ties both with *praxis* and with values. To put it another way, the values in the nouveau roman are entirely ad hoc and provisional.

Despite the antimimetic program of Robbe-Grillet and Ricardou, and despite the cultural debacle that this program entails, the novel has traditionally responded to a problematic

[5] Georg Lukacs, *The Theory of the Novel*, pp. 29–39.
[6] Erich Auerbach, *Mimesis*, pp. 4–5.
[7] Lukacs, *The Theory of the Novel*, pp. 124–26.
[8] Ibid., pp. 152–53.

realm of *praxis,* and the openness of its form has reflected the quest for values Lukacs talks about. In *Aspects of the Novel,* E. M. Forster accepts Abel Chevalley's definition of the novel as "a fiction in prose of a certain extent," qualifying that definition by saying that the extent should not be less than 50,000 words. He points out that no alternative definition will include *The Pilgrim's Progress, Marius the Epicurean, The Journal of the Plague Year, Zuleika Dobson, Rasselas, Ulysses,* and *Green Mansions,* or else will give reasons for their exclusion. Having placed Jane Austen and Thackeray in the middle of the "spongy tract" of fiction, he describes Poetry and History as chains of mountains that rise gradually on either side of the tract and Prophecy as a sea that bounds it on the third side. That sea, which Forster connects with *Moby-Dick,* he describes as follows: "Prophecy—in our sense—is a tone of voice. It may imply any of the faiths that have haunted humanity—Christianity, Buddhism, dualism, Satanism, or the mere raising of human love and hatred to such a power that their normal receptacles no longer contain them: but what particular view of the universe is recommended—with that we are not directly concerned."[9] Although prophecy is not a salient mode in the English novel, the ethical impulse I have described, the impulse to define oneself in relation to the world and the world in relation to the self, is present even in Dickens's books. Dickens, the great vaudevillian of English fiction, comes in *Bleak House* (and to some extent in *Great Expectations*) to locate the obsessive behavior of his grotesques in a society of corrupt and vain human institutions.

The problems raised by the novel which the formalist (in terms of artistic form) is incapable of dealing with have to do with its cultural coordinates. Let us consider a sampling of great novels: *Moll Flanders, Emma, The Red and the Black, The Possessed,* and *Ulysses.* On the axis of open-closed societies, it seems to me that *Moll Flanders* and *The Possessed*

[9] E. M. Forster, *Aspects of the Novel,* pp. 6, 125–26.

are aligned on the one hand, *Emma* and *Ulysses* on the other, with *The Red and the Black* somewhere in the middle.[10] That is, *Moll Flanders* and *The Possessed* reflect highly open societies. In the first case, making assumptions about the values operative in *Moll Flanders* is so difficult that it is almost impossible to know whether there is any overall irony in the book. Conjunctions of elements (like love and money) which we would consider ironic might very well have seemed more or less consistent to Defoe, who reflected the burgeoning commercial ethos of his age. In the second case a society in process of dissolution is viewed in apocalyptic terms. The pressure of ideology in *The Possessed*, the moral and emotional convulsions which it provokes in the individual, make it impossible to arrive at assured interpretations of surface action in the book. Dostoevsky's own ideology creates a structure that can find closure only in complete renewal. In *The Red and the Black* Julien Sorel's models for conduct—the French revolution and Napoleon—are dissonant with the current historical moment. Julien's defeat is a function both of his own jejune sentiments and of the sheer force he must expend in thrusting himself through a society that offers him no adequate arena for his energies. *Emma* gives more of the appearance of the closed society—that is, the moral economy of the book is so clear that Emma's rudeness to Miss Bates has a resonance in this book comparable to that of Shatov's murder in *The Possessed*. What is noticeable in *Emma*, however, and what distinguishes it from the closed society of epic, is Jane Austen's irony. Highbury is a society to which an intelligent person can accommodate himself, but the limitations of such a society are clearly foregrounded. *Ulysses* attempts an accommodation of the epic and the novel: The forms are immanent in the world that Joyce depicts, but they

[10] Note that *Emma*, which Forster finds somewhere in the center of English fiction, is at one end of the spectrum of world fiction. Austen is able to satirize norms which she values, but society is not a problem for her, as it is for Stendhal; it is a constant.

are self-consciously so. Between the naive epic of Homer and the self-conscious epic of Joyce lies the whole patrimony of western symbols.

When Tzvetan Todorov acknowledges that "an image of the narrator" (with a concomitant "image of the reader") is a crucial element in the reading of a novel, he raises the question, To what extent does our awareness of historical circumstances affect the image that we form of the narrator? Our uncertainty about this image, about the extent of congruence between the fictional narrator (Moll) and the implied narrator of the novel, makes a reading of *Moll Flanders* very problematic. It is noteworthy that Todorov, after a long descriptive account of *Les Liaisons Dangereuses,* moves into the notion of the relation between the internal laws peculiar to the novel and the conventional laws external to it. He sees the two systems as engaged in a process of mutual infraction: In *Les Liaisons Dangereuses* the laws internal to the novel are violated at the end by the laws of social context; in Dickens the laws of objective probability (which Todorov feels prevail in Dickens) are frequently violated by laws peculiar to the internal world of the novel, usually in the form of a deus ex machina.[11] Our position is that there is a subtle dialectic between the internal laws of the novel and the laws of the social context (among which I would include our scientific laws as well as our social conventions). If this dialectic is not apparent in the novel, there are two tendencies: If the internal pole does not seem to be present—that is, if the writer seems to be giving us a transcription of life—then the novel is a supplement to our limited experience, as broadening as a European tour; if the external pole is not present—that is, if we sense no mimetic responsibility in the novel—then the novel is only "a way of writing"[12] and has no function separate from that of a lyric poem. The attacks on time made by Barthes and Robbe-Grillet accom-

[11] Tzvetan Todorov, "Les catégories du récit littéraire," p. 151.
[12] Robbe-Grillet, *For a New Novel,* p. 44.

pany a subversion in the nouveau roman of the relation between subject and object, of the distinctions between tenses and between kinds of discourse (personal and narrative). Robbe-Grillet's works move toward an eternal present of writing.

In relation to Henry Green, let us note that the traditions of English thought have been less radical than those of Continental thought. In France and Germany, the bourgeoisie had to wage a long and bitter struggle for political power, and compromise with the nobility was impossible. In contrast, the evolution of the bourgeoisie in England was rather rapid and, despite the revolutions of 1648 and 1688, entailed a compromise with the nobility. Locke, Berkeley, and Hume wrote at a time when the bourgeoisie had already seized political power, while the bourgeoisie was still fighting at the time of Descartes in France and Kant in Germany. Although Kant, the English empiricists, and Descartes share a belief in individual rights and liberty, they differ as to how we may view the prospect of harmony among individuals. The French bourgeoisie posited a necessary accord based on a mathematical model. Since the English bourgeoisie was concerned with the real, not the a priori nature of this accord, they could surrender innate ideas in favor of their empirical associations: Instead of the moral stoicism of duty, the English are characterized by an epicurean utilitarianism. Because the Germans could share neither the illusion of a dogmatic rationalism nor an empirical skepticism, German thought aimed at overcoming a sick society through moral action. The English empirical tradition accounts in general for the less radical social vision one finds in English literature, as opposed to Continental literature. Lukacs's notion of the novel as entailing the thrust of a problematic individual against a problematic society is less persuasive in relation to what F. R. Leavis calls "the great tradition" than it is in relation to Continental literature. Even in George Eliot the idea of society is not probed as radically as it is by Stendhal and

Dostoevski. (The one exception to this generalization is D. H. Lawrence.)

The English empirical tradition accounts in particular for the epistemological reticence in Henry Green and for his final distrust of structure. That is, contemporary French writers like Jean Ricardou see the novel as subject to some of the same formal concerns present in poetry. This view of fiction is accompanied by a distrust of history that one does not find in English criticism. In *The Order of Things,* Michel Foucault claims that underlying the various inquiries a civilization engenders (in linguistic analysis, economics, physical science, and the like) is an *épistême* that determines the mode of inquiry. What Foucault cannot account for is how one gets from one *épistême* to another. In this sense both Foucault's book and Jacques Derrida's *De la grammatologie* have raised the question: What is the ontological status of structure? It becomes clear in Derrida, for example, that the *découpage* man commits on reality makes the real available to us but is without ontological status.[13] In Lévi-Strauss, myth—having its origins in a kind of *ur*-structure of the mind—admits of no accidents. Insofar as the novel moves toward the structuration of poetry, it too admits of no accidents. Whereas the traditional novel foregrounded the adventitious, the circumstantial, the nouveau roman fulfills that function on the one hand (in Robbe-Grillet's precise descriptions) and rejects it on the other (those descriptions are subject to textual manipulations that undermine their autonomy). Henry Green also pushes for structure, for the inevitability of each word at its point in a tight network, but he knows that structure is not all. As opposed to the kind of counter-anguish that one finds in Sartre and Camus (the absurd, the crack in the structure being our warrant of freedom), Green's respect for words is too great to allow him to transgress the necessary silence. Contrasting with the breaking down of tense distinctions and

[13] See Michel Foucault, *The Order of Things;* and Jacques Derrida, *De la grammatologie.*

differences in person ("I," "you," "he") in the nouveau roman, Green's novels maintain traditional shifts in tense and identify the speaker. If the nouveau roman, like the novels of Kafka and Beckett, is a radical response to the extreme reification of modern society, Green's more empirical response acts to reaffirm a place of human inwardness. The informing vision of the more radical works of Kafka, Beckett, and Robbe-Grillet breaks down the realms of subjective and objective, one realm appropriating the functions of the other. If subjectivity is all in Kafka, that subjectivity suffers from the same reification or automatization that characterizes a capitalist economy. Green's more empirical vision involves a sense of the homogeneity of totalitarian situations (ranging from the fascism of British public schools to an incomprehensible world war to the deadening uniformity of the civil service) and the resiliency that allows the individual to resist. For Green, as for W. H. Auden, school life is "an enlargement of the relationships which obtain between people in the world" (*Pack My Bag,* p. 17).

The problems of being, structure, and history, then, bring us to the problem of language. Man is an articulate animal in the most Latinate sense of the word: By articulating, dividing up reality, he makes it signify. The positivist critic emphasizes the instrumentality of language and the "reality" of reality. There is enough consensus, that is, about objective reality to free us from concerns about the arbitrary nature of language. In literature, consequently, his approach is to reduce the perspicuous language of the novel to the sociohistorical "realities" for which it stands. The structuralist critic, on the other hand, emphasizes the arbitrary aspects of "reality," or the "unreality" of language. Language is a system of relationships and values that does not reflect or represent reality but provides us with a grid with which we locate it. For Barthes literature explores the problematic of language. Classical literature, for example, exemplifies an arbitrary rationality of language, just as modern poetry exemplifies an arbitrary irrationality.[14] Similarly, the enumerations characteristic of Defoe's novels are not innocent or transparent: The quantitative vocabulary of Defoe's narrators reflects the reification of a burgeoning capitalist society and its concomitant mystification of language.

Philip Rahv says, "All that we can legitimately ask of a novelist in the matter of language is that it must be appropriate to the matter in hand. What is said must not stand in a contradictory relation to the way it is said, for that would dispel the illusion of life and with it the credibility of the fiction."[15] It is difficult to know how seriously Rahv takes "the illusion of life." Is he referring to a phenomenon such as the anecdotes actors in soap operas tell about receiving mail addressed to the characters whom they play, giving them advice, commiserating with them? The notion of appropriateness is not objectionable in itself; no one would claim that the language of a novel should be inappropriate to its fiction. However, Rahv seems to mean by "appropriate" something like the "economy of creative effort" that Victor Shklovsky combats in his essay "Art as Technique." This notion has to do with the efficiency with which a work of art brings one to the perceptions it intends to convey. Shklovsky distinguishes between "practical language" and "poetic language"; the first expedites our apprehension of the "matter," the second purposefully impedes that apprehension. Shklovsky points out that the processes of education and socialization train us to economize our perceptions, to extract from them what is useful for purposes of cognition: "The purpose of art is to impart the sensations of things as they are perceived and not as they are known. The technique of art is to make objects 'unfamiliar', to make forms difficult, to increase the difficulty and length of perception because the process of perception is an aesthetic end in itself and must be prolonged. Art is a

[14] Roland Barthes, *Critical Essays*, pp. 159–60.
[15] Philip Rahv, "Fiction and the Criticism of Fiction," p. 297.

way of experiencing the artfulness of an object; the object is not important."[16]

Language makes possible the purposeful dislocations of time that allow the formalist distinction between story and plot: the former is the action itself, the latter how one learns of the action. Of this distinction Shklovsky says, "The forms of art are explainable by the laws of art; they are not justified by their realism. Slowing the action of a novel is not accomplished by introducing rivals, for example, but by simply transposing parts. In so doing the artist makes us aware of the aesthetic laws which underlie both the transposition and the slowing down of the action."[17] This observation stands in contrast to Lessing's admiration of the care with which classical storytellers maintain the parallelism between the "signs or means of imitation" (narration) and the "objects" of imitation (the story or fiction). If modern storytellers engage in long descriptions that immobilize the story and foreground the narrative process itself, Homer converts even the description of Achilles's shield into a story: "Homer does not paint the shield finished, but in the process of creation. Here again he has made use of the happy device of substituting progression for coexistence, and thus converted the tiresome description of an object into a graphic picture of an action. We see not the shield but the divine master-workman employed upon it."[18] Lessing believes that, since fiction creates an illusion similar to that created by painting, the narrative process should be as perspicuous as possible. Although there is little

[16] Victor Shklovsky, "Art as Technique," p. 12. One is reminded of the agreement between Wordsworth and Coleridge regarding the *Lyrical Ballads:* Coleridge would try to make the supernatural or romantic seem familiar, and Wordsworth would try to excite a feeling analogous to the supernatural about everyday, familiar people and events. Wordsworth was to awaken the mind from the "lethargy of custom." See Samuel Taylor Coleridge, *Biographia Literaria,* in *Selected Poetry and Prose,* ed. Elisabeth Schneider, pp. 284–85.

[17] Shklovsky, "Art as Technique," p. 57.

[18] Gotthold Ephraim Lessing, *Laocoon,* p. 114.

temporal deformation in Green's works in the sense of events being displaced in time (the only real example of this transposition of events is *Caught*), there is a good deal of montage —the use of alternating scenes to give a sense of simultaneity. Recurring motifs also emphasize the synchronic dimension of his works. As we shall see in a later chapter, the fact that prose description can render only a few objects in a scene or a few aspects of one object disposes those objects to relationships much like the asentential relationships generated by rhyme. At the same time the perceptual whole is always less than the sum of its parts, since we tend to register events by perceiving one of a few of their parts or by perceiving contiguous events (by synecdoche or metonymy). In a sense, prose description defamiliarizes this signifying process, since it renders step by step and by addition the perceptual process that takes place simultaneously and by subtraction.

In terms of the "fit" between narrative and story, it would seem to be perfect in the case of direct discourse or dialogue. In this case mimesis would disappear, since we no longer have a *representation* of reality but an insertion of reality itself—the spoken word.[19] However, in a statement on nonrepresentational fiction, Green posits a contrary dialectical relationship between the dialogue in his books and dialogue in real life:

[19] Socrates' final prayer in the *Phaedrus,* where he asks for correspondence between the inner and the outer man, has to do with the relation between word and experience. In his polemic against the rhetoricians, Socrates is aiming at a "living word" that, as opposed to the opacity of rhetoric, generates a transparency between inner and outer. By "living word" I mean a word that can respond to questions, unlike the written eloquence of the rhetoricians. Plato's preference in the *Laws* (II. 658) for epic has to do in part with the fact that epic seems to involve less feigning than tragedy. For Aristotle, on the other hand, the norm is mimesis—a movement toward otherness rather than an accord between the inner and outer man. In this respect Aristotle's stress on action rather than thought in the *Poetics,* since thought would involve complete homogeneity between the signifier and the thing signified (*Poetics,* 6. 1450b).

"Non-representational" was meant to represent a picture which was not a photograph, nor a painting on a photograph, nor, in dialogue, a tape-recording. For instance the very deaf, as I am, hear the most astounding things all around them, which have not, in fact been said. This enlivens my replies until, through mishearing, a new level of communication is reached. My characters misunderstand each other more than people do in real life, yet they do so less than I. Thus when writing, I "represent" very closely what I see (and I'm not seeing so well now) and what I hear (which is very little) but I say it is "non-representational" because it is not necessarily what others see and hear.[20]

This lack of consensus, this denial of verisimilitude, is what characterizes the attacks on representational fiction we have discussed. It is what David Daiches means by observing that the modern novelist does not have a publicly shared standard of significance in his novels.

Another mode of defamiliarization that the Russian formalists discuss is manipulation of point of view. In this discussion they concentrate on the changes in language that such manipulation brings about (we recall that Henry James supplements the inadequate language of Maisie with his own). One example that Tomashevsky gives is Gulliver's arrival in the land of the Houyhnhnms, where he has to tell his master (a horse) about the mores of England's ruling class: "Compelled to tell everything with the utmost accuracy, he removes the shell of euphemistic phrases and fictitious traditions which justify such things as war, class strife, parliamentary intrigue, and so on. Stripped of their verbal justification and thereby defamiliarized, these topics emerge in all their horror. This criticism of the political system—nonliterary material—is artistically motivated and fully involved in the narrative.[21] Although Green is not interested in the peculiar refractions of events that writers like James and Ford Madox Ford achieve in their manipulation of point of view, he is

[20] Terry Southern, "The Art of Fiction XXII, Henry Green," p. 66.
[21] Boris Tomashevsky, "Thematics," p. 86.

concerned with the distance between the fictional narrator and his characters. A narrator may have a larger cognitive scope than his characters, the same cognitive scope, or less cognitive scope (the mystery novel is the best example of the last). Green's epistemological wariness, his sense that the novel should not violate the privacy of human inwardness, makes him increasingly reluctant to assume greater cognitive scope than his characters. As a matter of fact, in *Concluding* (one of his late novels) we know less at the end of the book than do some of the characters. The ambiguities of his cross-purpose dialogue and the intimations he achieves through description emphasize the oblique quality of communication.

Problems of language bring us to the shifting division between poetry and prose. In *Language of Fiction,* David Lodge polemicizes against viewing the novel in terms of more or less perfect translatability. What I mean by "perfect translatability" is as follows: Marx distinguishes between use value and exchange value. The former has to do with the quality of a product and consequently with the quality of the labor that produced it, whereas the latter has to do with the quantity of the product and the amount of labor that produced it. In aesthetic terms use value would refer to the qualities that individuate a work of art; exchange value would refer to the qualities that enable us to exchange one work of art for another. A clear example of the latter is the effort of Lévi-Strauss to show the relations of homology and inversion between various myths. The primary critical concern of Philip Rahv and Christopher Caudwell, moreover, is how persuasively the events of a novel translate into political, social, and economic realities. This is what Caudwell means when he says, "The poem and the story both use sounds which awake images of outer reality and affective reverberations; but in poetry the affective associations are organized by the structure of the language, while in the novel they are organized by the structure of the outer reality portrayed."[22] We have

[22] Christopher Caudwell, *Illusion and Reality,* p. 242.

noted the problem with this critical position even in relation to Defoe, whose fiction was described by Lamb as "like reading evidence in a court of Justice."[23] Defoe's language, far from being innocent, is as much a part of the subject of *Moll Flanders* as the heroine's career. David Lodge makes a similar point about a passage in Jane Austen: "It is indeed a logical passage; but such logic applied to human experience in fiction is not normative. It constitutes the special quality of Jane Austen's vision of experience, and is communicated to us through a special kind of language, language which is more than the transparent container of ideas."[24] But in arguing against the greater translatability of the novel, in arguing that there is no denotative level of language before the expressive activity of the novelist and that the experience of the novel is conveyed by "these words in this order," Lodge is misleading concerning the traditional mode of the novel. In view of his criticism of the modern apotheosis of the lyric as the premier poetic form, it is ironical that his derogation of problems of *praxis* reminds one of Mallarmé's notion that the lyrical poem is responsible only to its own silence.

"I have been one acquainted with the night," writes Robert Frost, and this line points up the particular kind of uncontextual situation involved in the poem as against prose discourse. What Jesperson calls "shifter words" (pronouns, certain adverbs of time and place) locate an absence of context that characterizes the poem, and the typographical space around a poem is emblematic of this absence. Who is the "I" in Frost's poem? What is the here of poetry? the now? All one can say is that the "I" is the speaker of the poetic utterance and that the adverbs relate to the act of utterance. If we think of a speaker encoding a message that another person will decode, thanks to a context to which the message refers and a code (language) which is common to both parties, one notes that the predominant poetic function of language is to

[23] Charles Lamb to Walter Wilson, 16 December 1822, quoted in Ian Watt, *The Rise of the Novel*, p. 34.

[24] David Lodge, *Language of Fiction*, p. 15.

focus on the message as such, whereas discursive prose emphasizes the context (social, moral, physical, or psychological) of the message.[25] One notes that Aristotle does not deal with the lyric form in the *Poetics,* where the element of *praxis* is primary. It is one thing to say with critics like Barthes, Robbe-Grillet, and Ricardou that one wants to liberate the novel from history, from its traditional pragmatic function. It is another to say that it has never really served such a function. The line between literature and nonliterature is constantly shifting, as sociologists and other researchers take over the documentary function that the realistic novel once served. Before we consider these changes in the language of the novel, let us consider the continuum of poetry and prose which Lodge mentions, but which he does not analyze.

Assume a continuum, the two poles of which are poetry and prose: The purest form we have of the former is the lyric poem and the purest form we have of the latter is the scientific treatise. The thrust of poetry is vertical. Even when a lyric poem has some narrative push, like Edwin Arlington Robinson's "Reuben Bright," the narrative movement is halted and renewed by each line ending and beginning, is reversed by the couplings (such as rhyme) that are generated by line position and that create the paradigmatic sense of the poem. Jakobson has pointed out that

> the poetic function projects the principle of equivalence from the axis of selection into the axis of combination. Equivalence is promoted to the constitutive device of the sequence. In poetry one syllable is equalized with any other syllable of the same sequence; word stress is assumed to equal word stress, as unstress equals unstress; prosodic long is matched with long, and short with short; word boundary equals word boundary, no boundary equals no boundary; syntactic pause equals syntactic pause, no pause equals no pause. Syllables are converted into units of measure, and so are morae or stresses.[26]

[25] Roman Jakobson, "Linguistics and Poetics," p. 299.
[26] Ibid., pp. 303–4.

Jakobson's observation that poetry and metalanguage mirror each other—in that the former uses equations to generate sequences and the latter uses sequences to generate equations—has been developed in a series of brilliant studies by Michael Riffaterre, who carefully demonstrates the high redundancy quotient of poetry. For Riffaterre a poem dramatizes the polarities of a matrix sentence (like "the rose is sick") by encoding these polarities in a temporal sequence. However much a poetic text proceeds syntactically and lexically, it keeps processing the same information.[27] The clearest model of this equational system is Wallace Stevens's "Metaphors of a Magnifico," where the poet's attempts to generate an equation fall into bare tautology and elliptical fragments.

Opposed to this sense of synchronicity in poetry, the novel is diachronic and linear in thrust. Closure is traditionally achieved by the passing of some character or characters from one set of circumstances to another that the novelist makes us anticipate. Although this anticipation implies a tautological aspect to novels as well as to poems, the problematic nature of time in the novel, as well as the complex system of mediators, pulls the novel away from the mode of wish fulfillment. Since prose does not project the "principle of equivalence" from "the axis of selection into the axis of combination," it is not under the same formal constraints as poetry to produce metaphorical closure. Contrasting with the redundancy quotient of poetry, prose will provide more progressive disclosure than retrogressive dramatization.

The Russian formalist Shklovsky sees *Tristram Shandy*—in its recognition that one can never really supply an adequate documentation of circumstances (one of the special properties of the novel)—as the most representative novel that we have.[28] One of the distinctive qualities of *Tristram Shandy* is

[27] See the following essays by Michael Riffaterre: "Interpretation and Descriptive Poetry"; "Le poème comme représentation"; and "The Self-Sufficient Text."

[28] Shklovsky, "Sterne's *Tristram Shandy*," p. 57.

its frustration of perhaps our primary expectation in the traditional novel—that we are going to get somewhere, from one moment in time to another, one set of circumstances to another. To some extent all novels work against this expectation: They suspend linear movement, progressive development, in order to defamiliarize our sense of how we know things. But a temporal push is a primary condition of the traditional novel. E. M. Forster points out in his discussion of the "story":

> So daily life, whatever it may be really, is practically composed of two lives—the life in time and the life by values—and our conduct reveals a double allegiance. "I only saw her for a few minutes, but it was worth it." There you have both allegiances in a single sentence. And what the story does is to narrate the life in time. And what the entire novel does—if it is a good novel—is to indicate the life by values as well. . . . It, also, pays a double allegiance. But in it, in the novel the allegiance to time is imperative: no novel could be written without it.[29]

The circumstantial particularity seen by Lukacs and others as characteristic of the novel is achieved by means of the anticipations that have been aroused by our sense of linear movement. In this, the novel is like the periodic sentence, which holds our attention through numerous qualifying clauses because of our sense of impending progressive movement. The poem, on the other hand, "will not declare itself"; it holds our attention through the expectations it arouses of reiteration.

A major problem in Lodge's consideration of fiction is that he is not sufficiently precise about the nature of language. He accepts a definition of style as revealing the freedom of the writer: "The stream of experience is the background against which 'choice' is a meaningful concept, in terms of which the phrase 'way of saying it' makes sense, though 'it'

[29] Forster, pp. 28–29.

is no longer a variable. Form and content are truly separate if 'content' is no bodiless idea, but the formless world stuff."[30] What this passage really describes is not so much literary style as language itself. The choices of the writer are limited by the horizon of his language, which has already submitted the "formless world stuff" to its own organization. The stuff of experience and the realm of *praxis* already have form before the writer begins to exercise his options. Given the fact that our experience is articulated by what Derrida calls an "archi-écriture," the question is, To what extent are we aware of this function of language in ordinary thought and discourse? Do we not, in fact, tend to believe that the structure of our language reflects reality, that there is something peculiarly natural about the subject-predicate order of English sentences? How often are we aware of the arbitrary nature of the grid language throws over reality in order to render it meaningful?

Given the common denominator of a language mediating *all* experience, can we distinguish realms of language which render that mediating function more or less patent? Poetry has always had the function of denaturalizing language. The *découpage* of poetry is emblematic of the peculiar quality of language: that its structure is separable from that which it structures. If ordinary discourse tends to delude us with the idea that the elements of language are self-evident since they refer to extra-linguistic elements, poetic language emphasizes the basic principle of language—that the element is determined by the system it presupposes. In this sense poetry does address itself to *logos*, if by *logos* we mean the informing principle of language. Despite Lodge's distinction between ordinary language and literary language (in the case of the latter, the "ordinary entailments are cut" in the sense that we do not question the truth or falsehood of literary statements), the language of the novel and ordinary language are

[30] Richard Ohmann, "Prologomena to the Analysis of Prose Style," quoted in Lodge, *Language of Fiction*, p. 64.

often homogeneous. At least in English, where we do not have the French *passé simple,* the formal properties of fictional language are often mistakable for those of ordinary language. "He stepped into a department store after lunch" could just as well be a real-life proposition as a sentence from a story. It is this homogeneity, as a matter of fact, that is attacked by Barthes, Robbe-Grillet, and Ricardou, who want literature to contest the false transparency of the anecdote.

In fiction the story or anecdote manifests characteristics that deemphasize the mediating function of language. The pronouns "I" and "you" refer neither to reality nor to objective positions in space and time, but to instances of discourse which contain them. "I" signifies that person who emits the instance of discourse containing the word "I." "You" signifies that person addressed in the present instance of discourse containing the word "you." Their role is to convert language into discourse, into an intersubjective process. Shifters like "here," "now," "today," "yesterday," "in three days" are also defined in terms of the moment of discourse. The traditional story or anecdote is characterized by the use of the third person, which does not partake of the intersubjective process but refers to real objects, historical times and places. Whereas "I" and "you" are empty signs filled by the instance of discourse, the third person is an abbreviated substitute ("*John* has won a scholarship; *he* is very happy"). Shifters like "there," "then," "the same day," and "the next day" also refer to a nonsubjective situation. They are historical counters. A similar situation prevails in terms of tense: The epic past tense gives the impression of no one speaking, of events telling themselves. Shifts to the present or future tenses are signs of a shift from story to discourse.[31] If the "realistic" novelist emphasized the referential function of language, if he worked at creating a sense of congruence between the third person mode and the socio-historical context he was evoking, modern

[31] Émile Benveniste, *Problèmes de linguistique générale,* pp. 237–57.

novelists like Joyce, Kafka, and the nouveau romanists emphasize the intrasystemic functions of language. Analyzing the parallelism between narrative and story (which gives the illusion that events are not being mediated by language), Jean Ricardou points out that a rupture of the parallelism in the modern novel foregrounds the axis of narration at the expense of the axis of the story. The alibi of the anecdote is abandoned, and "one sees how the novel ceases to be the writing of a history in order to become the history of a writing."[32] In Kafka's *The Trial*, for example, Joseph K. is arrested by order of a Tribunal, but this familiar image of justice is subverted by that individual's strange behavior. As Marthe Robert points out, Kafka's books proceed from a kind of semantic contradiction: Joseph K. feels arrested and everything takes place *as if* he were arrested; Kafka complains in his *Letter to His Father* that he is treated like a parasite, and the "like" is suppressed in "Metamorphosis."[33] Just as "*I* promise" is an act, whereas "*he* promises" is a description, Kafka's works are enactments of the inner life. In *Finnegans Wake*, the deemphasis of story in favor of narrative (or discourse) brings the novel to the vanishing point.

As the novel moves toward the poetic pole, where the "fit" between message and context becomes more problematic, the language of the novel is characterized by figures that spatialize the language of poetry. These figures, which exploit the possibility that reading creates of rereading, foreground the literary function of language as distinguished from its referential function. A figure involves the presence of one signifier making us aware of the absence of another signifier. Whereas a simple and ordinary expression has no form, the figure is characterized by an internal space or *écart* between sign and sense. In Hart Crane's "the eyes walking the straight road toward thunder," for example, "eyes" and "thunder"

[32] Ricardou, *Problèmes du nouveau roman*, p. 166.
[33] Marthe Robert, *Kafka*, pp. 106–7.

evoke the absence of other terms. Gérard Genette says of this process, "A sign or a sequence of linguistic signs forms only a line, and this linear form is the business of grammarians. Rhetorical form is a surface, that which the two lines of present signifier and absent signifier delimit."[34]

While examining the practice of Henry Green, we shall discern two basic kinds of figures: syntactic figures, which have roughly to do with what Chomsky calls "agrammaticalness"; and discursive figures, which have to do with the staggered relations between discourse and story. (Chapter III will deal for the most part with the former, Chapter IV with the latter.) Generally, these figures are motivated by the desire for defamiliarization. Genette points out that when one uses the word "sail" to refer to a sail, this significance is arbitrary and conventional. It is also abstract, since the word designates a concept and not a thing, and unambiguous, a simple denotation. But using the word "sail" for ship is richer and more complex. It is ambiguous, since "sail" designates both sail and ship; it is concrete and motivated, since it designates the ship by a material detail and since it chooses that detail rather than another (like "mast" or "rigging").[35] Undermining what the Russian formalists call the "algebra of perception," the figure causes us to *realize* by means of a sensory detour the object of recognition. Ricardou's notion of description as "a machine to disorient my vision"[36] involves both the general notion of defamiliarization (which is really a defamiliarization of ordinary discourse, ordinary designation) and the more particular notion of "openness" or "indetermination." Umberto Eco takes the position that an artistic form is an "epistemological metaphor" revealing the manner in which science or at least contemporary culture views reality. Positing a structural analogy between the scientific method and the poetics of an era, Eco points to the structural analo-

[34] Gérard Genette, *Figures,* pp. 209–10.
[35] Ibid., p. 219.
[36] Ricardou, *Problèmes du nouveau roman,* p. 18.

gies between works of art (like serial or aleatory music) or aesthetic theory (contemporary aesthetic notions of openness and ambiguity) on the one hand and the epistemological assumptions underlying quantum physics, multivalent logic, and modern psychology and phenomenology on the other. In Einstein's time-space continuum, the infinite possibilities of relative experience are contained by invariant conditions expressed by differential equations. Similarly, the work of art is open within the framework of a "field" (Barthes would say "structure") of relations.[37] The use of figures in the modern novel recalls Valéry's animadversions on the traditional novel: "Perhaps it would be interesting, just once, to write a work which at each juncture would show the diversity of solutions that can present themselves to the mind and from which it chooses the unique sequel to be found in the text. To do this would be to substitute for the illusion of a unique scheme which imitates reality that of the possible-at-each-moment, which I think more truthful."[38] The figures in Green's novels allude to this "possible-at-each-moment," undermining the "innocence" or univocalness of the anecdote.

[37] Umberto Eco, *L'Oeuvre ouverte*, pp. 15–37.
[38] Paul Valéry, *The Art of Poetry*, p. 104.

III

The Norms of Language

The perfection of Diction is for it to be at once clear and not mean. The clearest indeed is that made up of the ordinary words for things, but it is mean.

[Aristotle, *Poetics* (trans. Ingram Bywater), 22. 1458a. 18–20. In Aristotle, *Rhetoric and Poetics* (New York: Modern Library, 1954]

In his book *The Novels of Henry Green,* Edward Stokes gives a comprehensive survey of the stylistic traits of Green's books. Toward this survey, which is supported by statistical tabulation, Max Cosman expresses a vulgar condescension by no means atypical in literary criticism:

> But integrating the mass of material he does have, and, in addition, tabulating and measuring for himself Green's elements of expression, Mr. Stokes comes to a host of conclusions, the most characteristic of which are highly idiosyncratic. "*Loving,*" says one of them, "has more preterit verbs than any other novel except *Living.*" "*Blue,*" goes a second, "is actually the most frequently occurring color in *Caught.*" "Natural imagery," points out still another, "is more plentiful in *Concluding* than in any novel since *Party Going.*" And a fourth, apropos of sentence-lengths, reports that "*Back* is much closer to *Loving, Nothing,* and *Doting* than to the other novels."
>
> Such information may well cause some readers to feel as Walt Whitman did when he heard a certain learned astronomer anatomize the mystery of the stars. It had no such effect, however, on Mr. Green. Quite the contrary. It has impressed him very favorably.[1]

The title of Cosman's article is "The Elusive Henry Green," and Cosman seems determined to keep Green that way. Quoting

[1] Max Cosman, "The Elusive Henry Green," p. 474.

the results of tabulations out of context can always make them seem gratuitous or idiosyncratic, but one wonders by what standard Cosman denigrates these conclusions. He has presumably read them in context, and yet he gives no indication in his brief article as to why they are not pertinent to a general description and evaluation of Green's works. Cosman seems to be saying: Most people look at frogs from the outside; they see frogs as wholes having a certain shape, color, and means of locomotion. The biologist who piths the frog comes to certain idiosyncratic conclusions about it because he violates the frog's integrity. If one is interested, however, in knowing more about frogs than can be derived from everyday observation, the biologist's analyses are essential. They also reveal much about the relationship of frogs to other animals. In the same way, Stokes's methods reveal qualities of Green's books that would remain implicit otherwise, and provide means of testing our intuitions about these qualities. Besides telling us something about the way we read, they provide more explicit means by which we can compare the qualities of Green's novels with those of other novels. Only if the critic's role is restricted to measuring a book by the moral, social, or psychological commonplaces it evokes or is restricted to the "oohing and aahing" mode of evaluation, does structural analysis become irrelevant.

Before adumbrating Stokes's general findings, let me place the above quotations in context. When Stokes points out that there are more preterit verbs in *Loving* than in any other novel by Green except *Living*, he goes on to say that there are fewer verbs of any other kind in *Loving* than in any of Green's novels. In comparing *Loving* with *Party Going*, for example, he sets up the table shown on page 51. Stokes concludes from these figures (and from another table giving percentages from all of Green's novels except *Blindness*) that in *Loving* Green restricts himself more than he does in his other books to the "fictive present" (the preterit), to action and observable be-

		Party Going	*Loving*
1	Preterit (type "did")	319	388
2	"Had done" type	70	28
3	"Might (etc.) do" type	65	18
4	"Was doing" type	43	21
5	"Did . . . do" type	27	8
6	"Do/does" type	24	3
7	Others	37	17
	Total	585	483

Reprinted, by permission of the publisher, from Edward Stokes, *The Novels of Henry Green* (London: The Hogarth Press, 1959), p. 227. Copyright © Edward Stokes 1959.

havior, and that the past in this book is not the backdrop it is in *Party Going*. While the absence of the present tense indicates a scarcity of commentary and of interior monologue, the third line of the chart indicates "the greater decisiveness, concreteness, and immediacy of *Loving*, compared with *Party Going;* or, to put the distinction more fairly, the large number of verbs compounded of 'might' and similar auxiliaries indicates that the interest of *Party Going* lies much more in the relationships between actions and in motives, than in the actions themselves."[2] The fact that Stokes's interpretation of the data may be questionable does not invalidate the data's suggestiveness.

I have quoted Stokes's last observation because it is insufficiently subtle. Although there is greater interior presentation in *Party Going* than in any of Green's other novels, *Party Going* raises the question of the exhaustibility of personality more cogently than any of the other novels. Moreover, although the "might do" grammatical mode (which includes also the auxiliaries "may," "must," "would," "could," and

[2] Edward Stokes, *The Novels of Henry Green*, pp. 226–27.

"should") implies a relation between two moments in time, it does not necessarily imply a relation between two actions or an interest in motives. The mode expresses anticipation or potentiality, and the only clear case of its connecting two actions is in an "if . . . then" (or comparable) clausal structure. Putting this question aside, however, the observations which arise from data of this sort should make us test more explicitly our intuitions about what we are reading.

When Stokes points out that blue is the color occurring most frequently in *Caught,* he is rigorously examining a phenomenon that is more salient in Green than in any other author I have read: the sense that certain kinds of experiences are being registered on a kind of spectroscope. If we recall Susan Sontag's observation that "form—in its specific idiom, style—is a plan of sensory imprinting,"[3] we see how important the frequency of certain colors is in Green's books for the imprinting of certain scenes. This mnemonic concern applies also to the incidence of natural imagery in Green's books.

Finally, sentence length, as well as sentence structure, reveals the resistance an author's style offers to the progressive movement of the novel. If we assume that the attention span an author typically demands in his sentences reflects the amount of rational control he is attempting to exert over his context, then alignments among Green's novels in terms of sentence length can be revealing.

At this point let us summarize some of Stokes's findings: While the basis of Green's style is the short, syntactically simple sentence, kinds of sentence sequences vary from book to book. For example, *Back* is characterized more than any of the other novels by long sequences of short sentences. *Party Going* manifests a relative homogeneity of sentence lengths. Although *Caught* and *Concluding* have about the same dis-

[3] Susan Sontag, *Against Interpretation,* p. 43.

tribution of sentence lengths, differences in subject matter and technique make us more aware of both the very short and the long, elaborate sentences in *Caught* than we are in *Concluding*.[4] Stokes's interpretations of his statistics vary in cogency. He is correct, for example, when he observes that in *Back* the extended sequences of short sentences reflect the damage from which the central character is suffering.[5] But his supposition that the homogeneity of sentence lengths in *Party Going* is appropriate to the unity of time and place and to the homogeneity of the group involved, falls into the fallacy of imitative form.[6] Attempting to imitate syntactically a mode of awareness, a movement of consciousness, is appropriate; using a syntax which is in some way appropriate to a thing (like a homogeneous group) or a condition (unity of time and place) is at best only an affectation. Our analysis of Green's syntactic figures is an analysis of how prose makes conspicuous the act of awareness.

Henry Green's second novel, *Living*, which is about factory life in Birmingham, reveals a writer rebelling against the journeyman prose of contemporaries like Waugh and Isherwood and groping toward a more conspicuous style. As Stokes points out, *Living* is characterized by the partial extirpation of the definite article; frequent omissions of "there"; numerous fragmentary, verbless sentences; frequent inversions and distortions of normal word order; repetitions; the use of a redundant "so" in comparisons; an occasional use of "like" instead of "as if" or "as though"; and numbers not spelled out but given as Arabic numerals.[7] The most talked about of these stylistic devices has been Green's elisions, which he describes as follows: "I wanted to make that book as taut and spare as possible to fit the proletarian life I was then lead-

[4] Stokes, *The Novels of Henry Green*, pp. 202–29.
[5] Ibid., pp. 229–31.
[6] Ibid., p. 203.
[7] Ibid., pp. 196–98.

ing. So I hit on leaving out the articles. I still think it effective, but would not do it again. It may now seem, I'm afraid, affected." When asked, "Do you think that an elliptical method like that has a function other than, as you say, suggesting the tautness and spareness of a particular situation?" Green replied, "I don't know, I suppose the more you leave out, the more you highlight what you leave in. . . ."[8]

Undermining Green's mimetic explanation of this prose mannerism is the fact that he does not assume a luxurious prose when dealing with the rich in *Living*, *Party Going*, *Doting*, and *Nothing*. In fact, these ellipses occur in scenes dealing with the wealthy Duprets in *Living* and recur in *Party Going*. Moreover, some of Green's other mannerisms in *Living*, such as inversion and redundancy, cannot be explained by reference to the spareness of proletarian life. Whatever mimesis Green thought he was indulging in, the primary motivation behind these devices was an interest in English prose as an instrument of awareness. That is, it *is* something of an affectation to say that one is going to omit the articles in one's sentences in order to reflect the spare material circumstances in one's book. It is not uninteresting (whether one is successful or not) to say that one is going to omit these articles in order to foreground nouns in an unusual way. The omission of articles can have three effects:

1. It can give the effect of changing the status of common nouns to proper nouns. That is, the removal of articles (especially the indefinite article) removes an object (or person) from a category of objects (or persons) and stresses its singleness. The kind of consciousness reflected is primitive, unabstracting.

2. It can give the effect of making the noun more generic —unmodified "bird" becomes "birds," member becomes species. As we shall see in *Party Going*, that species then becomes a member of a genus which is difficult to define be-

[8] Terry Southern, "The Art of Fiction XXII, Henry Green," p. 73.

cause it is a mode of consciousness.

3. A third effect can result from the rearrangement of word order as well as from ellipses: a closer packing together (and thus a greater conspicuousness) of the most salient words of the sentence. Of this last effect especially, and of Green's mannerisms generally, Philip Toynbee states that Green was obviously averse to the looseness of modern English but that his solution in *Living* was mistaken. "It is true that a great fault of current speech lies in the proliferation of superfluous and meaningless sounds. . . . Some severity is needed. But 'the' is both an innocent and a useful word and to concentrate so heavy a gun against it seems a curious misdirection of this writer's fire power." He feels that the omission of the definite article and the emphatic inversions are self-conscious and irritating, especially in view of the ordinary statements that are being made.[9]

Toynbee's judgment is too summary, especially if one recalls W. H. Auden's problems in "Spain, 1937," with "the," which thuds throughout the poem. Although "the" has a syncopated vowel, one cannot hurry through the consonants. In order to deemphasize the article, Auden finally uses it as a feminine line ending.[10] In *Living* one can discern two kinds of motivation for Green's elisions of the definite article and of the nonadverbial "there": to convey a certain kind of awareness—of the immediacy of impressions and of the particularity of nouns rather than of their class; and to exercise control over prose cadence. In this sentence, "In the foundry was now sharp smell of burnt sand" (p. 34), the elision of "there" increases the immediacy of the impression. In another passage, "This man scooped gently at great shape cut down in black sand in great iron box. He was grimed with

[9] Philip Toynbee, "The Novels of Henry Green," pp. 491–92.

[10] Auden attributes this problem with the article to his interest in German. See the preface to his *Collected Shorter Poems, 1927–1957*, p. 16.

the black sand" (p. 4), the elision of the articles again makes the impressions more immediate, whereas the inclusion of the article in the last sentence creates a rhythm that better rounds off the section: "Hĕ wăs grímed wĭth thĕ bláck sánd" brings us to rest more effectively than "Hĕ wăs grímed with bláck sánd" after the heavy packing of stresses in the previous sentence. Typographical space follows this passage, and we move into a new scene. In order to give more credibility to this argument, let us examine Green's attentiveness to prose cadence in more detail.

Some of the redundancy in Green's prose has to do with prose rhythm. Like the song into which characters in O'Casey's plays sometimes burst, Green's prose rhythm serves to heighten certain moments. The epigraph to *Living*, which is extracted from a scene in which Mrs. Eames speculates about her child, is an example of such heightening: "As these birds would go where so where would this child go?" This sentence scans as follows (with the heavy pause after "where"): ˘´´˘´´˘´´˘´´, the first module exerting pressure on the second to accent "would" instead of "this." The phrase "ănd nów tíme ĭs passĭng nów" (p. 260), where "is" acts as a hinge connecting two different three-syllable modules, is a second example. (Let us note to the Satanic reader that the first module cannot exert the same pressure on the second module in this case because one cannot accept the second syllable of "passing.") "Wăs lów wáilĭng lów ĭn hĕr éars" (p. 108) includes an antispast and a choriamb (a kind of negative reiteration)—as equivalent units not of time but of energy. As these examples show, the redundant syllables call attention to the configurations of syllables in a way that normal prose does not. Similarly, careful variations of sentence length and inversions and other distortions of word order attract attention to the cadence of the sentence and to the larger cadence of the paragraph. Take this paragraph, for example:

Evening. Was spring. Heavy blue clouds stayed over above. In small back garden of villa small tree was with yellow buds. On table in back room daffodils, faded, were between ferns in a vase. Later she spoke of these saying she must buy new ones and how nice were first spring flowers.

[P. 11.]

A gradual expansion of the sentence unit gives a distinctive and pleasing cadence to the paragraph. The inversion in the sentence, "Mr. Bridges went down through works in Birmingham till Tupe he found" (p. 111), also draws attention to cadence. The following paragraph illustrates a number of possibilities:

Water dripped from tap on wall into basin and into water there. Sun. Water drops made rings in clear coloured water. Sun in there shook on the walls and ceiling. As rings went out round trembling over the water shadows of light from sun in these trembled on walls. On the ceiling.

[P. 40.]

First of all, the two sentence fragments generate a distinctive prose cadence in the paragraph, in somewhat the way the short lines in Herbert's "Easter" give cadence to the verse,

Rise heart; thy Lord is risen. Sing his praise
Without delayes,
Who takes thee by the hand, that thou likewise
With him may rise:
That, as his death calcined thee to dust,
His life may make thee gold, and much more, just.[11]

Second, the varying sentence lengths have a descriptive effect comparable to the varying range of camera shots in the movies. "Sun" and "on the ceiling" seem to generate a sud-

[11] See *The Poems of George Herbert*, p. 36.

den zoom-lens close-up, whereas the rest of the description seems to be at a middle distance. Finally, the penultimate sentence impedes our forward movement in various ways. The lack of a comma between "water" and "shadows" makes us pause because we are not sure at first glance where one clause ends and the other begins. Although prose is not usually thought to be for the ear in the way poetry is, we do subvocalize when we are not reading very quickly, and the omission of the article before "sun" then combines with the preponderance of monosyllabic words to slow down our reading. The phrase "in these" makes us hesitate also, since we are not immediately sure what the reference is. In summary, there is a careful control of reading tempo in this paragraph, which is a sort of set piece, a moment of intensified perception.

Green is experimenting in *Living* with methods of energizing English prose and of making it a more expressive instrument of awareness. Some of the ellipses in the book remind one of the shock Green experienced when he entered factory life, ". . . it was an introduction to indisputable facts at last . . ." (*Pack My Bag*, p. 236). The elision of "filler" words makes one's awareness of those facts more immediate and particular (the elisions do not imitate in any sense the relative spareness of material circumstances).[12] What one can obect to in *Living* are occasional lapses in tact. The stripped style seems inappropriate in the following passage, which describes a scene between wealthy Mrs. Dupret and her son:

She pushed button of bell; this was in onyx. She laid hand by it on table and diamonds on her rings glittered together with white metal round onyx button under the electric light. Electric light was

[12] The best example we have in American poetry of this celebration of the fact is Ralph Waldo Emerson's "Hamatreya":

> Bulkeley, Hunt, Willard, Hosmer, Meriam, Flint,
> Possessed the land which rendered to their toil
> Hay, corn, roots, hemp, flax, apples, wool and wood.
> [ll. 1–3]

like stone. He was cut short by her. He was hurt at it. He kept silence then.

[P. 37.]

Whose awareness, or what quality of awareness, is being evoked in this scene? Green seems to be imitating himself. The worst errors in tact occur in his inversions of syntax, which sometimes distract rather than heighten or please: "You were to him speaking, and he began quietly answering, then, suddenly, he was acting, sincere in feeling, but acting, and words were out pouring, fine sentiments fine" (p. 113).

In Green's next book, *Party Going*, he develops a surer control over these stylistic devices.

Take the opening paragraphs of *Party Going:*

Fog was so dense, bird that had been disturbed went flat into a balustrade and slowly fell, dead, at her feet.

There it lay and Miss Fellows looked up to where that pall of fog was twenty foot above and out of which it had fallen, turning over once. She bent down and took a wing then entered a tunnel in front of her, and this had DEPARTURES lit up over it, carrying her dead pigeon.

No one paid attention, all were intent and everyone hurried, nobody looked back. Her dead pigeon then lay sideways, wings outspread as she held it, its dead head down towards the ground. She turned and she went back to where it had fallen and again looked up to where it must have died for it was still warm and, everything explained, she turned once more into the tunnel back to the station.

She thought it must be dirty with all that fog and wondered if it might not be, now it was dead, that it had fleas and they would come out on the feathers of its head but she did not like to look as there might have been blood. She remembered she had seen that with rabbits' ears when they had been shot and she remembered that swallows were most verminous of all birds—how could it have died she wondered and then decided that it must be washed.

As Miss Fellows penetrated through at leisure and at last stepped out under a huge vault of glass—and here people hurriedly crossed her path and shuttled past on either side—Miss Crevy and her young man drove up outside and getting out were at once part of all that movement. And this affected them, for if they also had to engage in one of those tunnels to get to where they were going it was not for them simply to pick up dead birds and then wander through slowly. . . .

[Pp. 7–8.]

Unlike its particularizing effect in *Living*, the elision of articles before "fog" and "bird" gives these words a vague, generic quality. Encountering more than a particular fog or a particular bird, one is encountering "fogs" and "birds," which, occurring in various contexts throughout the book, become signals for certain kinds of awareness. As we shall see, the sense of weightlessness in these opening sentences is reinforced by Green's flat, paratactic style. In the first paragraph note that the correlative conjunction "that" is elided before "bird" as well as the article. The chiasmus "went flat" and "slowly fell" gives a slow motion effect as it delays the verb "fell." "Dead," surrounded by commas, further retards the action of the sentence. Finally, the pseudo-anaphoric "her" intensifies our sense of uncertainty.

The flat paratactic style of the opening paragraphs creates a sense of equality among all elements of the sentence. There is little deemphasizing of elements by subordination or by quickening of tempo, whereas emphasis is created by agrammatical devices. In paragraph two, for example, the imbalance of the two coordinate clauses stresses the short clause "there it lay," which is also foregrounded by its redundancy. This use of redundancy is characteristic of Green. At the end of the first chapter, we read, "Once free of them she went to where he had shown her and, partly because she felt so much better now, she retrieved her dead pigeon done up in brown paper" (p. 13). The redundant "done up in brown paper" is a suggestive and ominous detail at the end of this sentence and at the end of the chapter. In Jean Cohen's terms, the use of this redundant detail in the position of a restrictive phrase is agrammatical and forces us to find affective reasons for its use.[13] "Carrying her dead pigeon" is also foregrounded partly by its redundancy (we know that she is carrying the pigeon), partly by its position at the end of the sentence, and partly by its occurrence after the awkwardly inserted "and this had DEPARTURES lit up over it." Finally, the word "departures" is foregrounded typographically as well as by its occurrence in a phrase that would normally be subordinated but is coordinated in this sentence. Throughout the book these typographically foregrounded signs act as ominous signals, much in the way that Jean Luc Godard's signs act in his films.

One notes the use of asyndeton (another of Green's general mannerisms) in the opening sentence of paragraph three. Its use is carried over to the next sentence, the three units of which are given more autonomy than would be the case in another context. They seem three independent units (as in the first sentence) instead of one independent unit and two dependent ones. In the last sentence we have an emphatic use of the pseudo-organizational "and," as well as the use of a distracted and distracting "for" which seems to explain something but does not. The "everything explained" is a cryptic qualifying phrase which implies that more has taken place than we are aware of.

The fourth paragraph is packed with verbs compounded of "might" and similar auxiliaries: "must be," "might not be," "would come out," "might have been," "how could it have died," and "must be washed." These auxiliaries stress the sense of latent possibilities in the situation, possibilities which are obliquely rendered throughout the rest of the book. This paragraph also shows that although the norm with Green is the short, syntactically simple sentence, he is also master of the run-on sentence and, to a lesser extent, of the syntactically involute sentence. The lack of commas and the accommodating quality of "and" create a bluntness of discrimination which we shall discuss further.

[13] See Jean Cohen, *Structure du langage poétique*, pp. 139–63.

As we have noted, the exaggerated paratactic style of these opening paragraphs suspends the ordinary discriminations that sentences make by subordination, but subtle and unexpected emphases are provided by the sentence organization, use of auxiliaries, typology, redundancy, and elision. These devices generate figures by frustrating our normal syntactic expectations—by coordinating clauses that seem to demand subordination, by inverting the usual sentence order, by undermining the grammatical determination of nouns, by violating the privileges of certain grammatical positions, by using auxiliaries to subvert the indicative mode, and by isolating words typographically. These syntactic detours force us to explore their motivation. One recalls that in *The Good Soldier* Ford Madox Ford, having to convey both the obtuseness of the narrator and the true facts of the narrator's situation through a first-person narration, conveys both the refraction of events and the events themselves. In *Party Going* the syntactic detours suggest a similar disorder of perception and appreciation that we must remedy by the figures that carry *our* perception and appreciation. We respond to the peculiar syntax of the first sentence of the book by positing absent terms to which "fog" and "bird" allude. Similarly, we resolve the displacement caused by Green's use of redundant epithets by seeing the redundant detail ("done up in brown paper") as the present term of a metaphor.

The fifth paragraph illustrates a device similar to the use of redundancy in its occasional suggestiveness. The sentence "And this affected them, for if they also had to engage in one of those tunnels to get to where they were going it was not for them simply to pick up dead birds and then wander through slowly," is peculiarly pedantic. The suggestiveness of this pedantry comes from one's trying to figure out what question this sentence would be an appropriate answer to. If it is not for them "simply to pick up dead birds and then wander through slowly," whom *is* it for? This use of pedantry recurs later in the book:

Now both Julia and Angela had kissed their young men when these had been cross, when Mr. Adams had made off down in the station and when Max had stopped chasing Julia to sit in his chair.
People, in their relations with one another, are continually doing similar things but never for similar reasons.

[P. 114.]

As we shall see later, this pedantry deflates the solemn weighing of motives that characterizes the conventional novel. Another effect of the fifth paragraph is to draw our attention to the use of prepositions and pointing adverbs. One reason prepositions and adverbs do so much work in these opening pages is that they are foregrounded against the grid of non-relational "ands." In the context of fog, moreover, we become sensitized to certain movements (up and down, into and through) and to certain positions (in and on, inside and outside). At the beginning our first orientation in this fog (both descriptive and syntactic) is up and down: "*up* to where that pall of fog" and "*down toward* the ground." Then one moves "*into* the tunnel," "*back to* the station"; one "engage[s] *in* one of those tunnels" and "wander[s] *through*." Later in the book one becomes aware of the great difference between "drowning *in* their depths" (as do Robin and Miss Fellowes) and "clinging together *on* these depths" (as do Thomson and Emily). These positional indications accompany a parody of the Dantesque vertical stages—underground, ground level, and above ground. The vault of the railroad station covers everyone, whether he is underground (as Miss Fellowes and the two mortuary nannies are at the beginning), at ground level (the crowd in the station), or above ground (the party-goers). That vault cannot be seen by those underground; it looks green to those at ground level; and it looks blue to those closer to it, in rooms above the crowd. We shall see that this chromatic shift is always significant in the economy of Green's books.

Green's paratactic style accommodates the seriatim quality of literary description, what Ricardou calls the "essential deviation" between the object of perception and the object of description.[14] Although this deviation is a general property of literary description, particular literary descriptions exert more or less pressure against it. Our attention is strained in proportion to the number of units we are forced to keep in suspension and in relation to one another as we move through the sentence. This mnemonic strain is characteristic of the late Jamesian style, where James attempts to spatialize psychological description, to synchronize what must necessarily be presented in a linear, temporal, and progressive mode.[15] A similar problem characterizes the physical descriptions of Robbe-Grillet's books, particularly those of *Jealousy.* The strategy of *Jealousy* is as follows: at the beginning of the book, Robbe-Grillet gives us a map of a house and its environs. He also gives us an index of significant moments in the book ("Now the shadow of the column . . . [p. 39]," "The brush descends the length . . . [p. 66]," etc.). His literary descriptions then dissolve these objects and spatial relations into linear movements. Our attempt to respatialize these elements is the strain to which we referred above. As in James, we must reread to overcome the temporal. Robbe-Grillet in fact provides literal rereadings, i.e., repetitions of descriptive units, which parody our rereadings of the same passage. Henry Green's "ands" (and to some extent the other conjunctions, "so," "for," "but") parody the linear character of literary description, as does his use of asyndeton. We do not suffer the mnemonic discomfort of James's involute sen-

[14] Jean Ricardou, *Problèmes du nouveau roman,* p. 19.

[15] Note Max Beerbohm's parody of James's late style in "The Guerdon": "That it hardly was, that it all bleakly and unbeguilingly *wasn't* for 'the likes' of him—poor decent Stamfordham—to rap out queries about the owner of the to him unknown and unsuggestive name that had, in these days, been thrust on him with such a wealth of commendatory gesture, was precisely what now, as he took, with his prepared list of New Year *colifichets* and whatever, his way to the great gaudy palace, fairly flicked his cheek with the sense of his having never before so let himself in, as he ruefully phrased it, without letting anything, by the same token, out." In *Parodies,* p. 147. The italics are Beerbohm's.

tences or of Robbe-Grillet's spatial dissolutions; what we do experience, however, is the discomfort of disorientation.[16]

Green does move occasionally into passages that are more stylistically complex, the longest and most elaborate of which is:

Looking down then on thousands of Smiths, thousands of Alberts, hundreds of Marys, woven tight as any office carpet or, more elegantly made, the holy Kaaba soon to set out for Mecca, with some kind of design made out of bookstalls and kiosks seen from above and through one part of that crowd having turned towards those who were singing, thus lightening the dark mass with their pale lozenged faces; observing how this design moved and was alive where in a few lanes or areas people swayed forward or back like a pattern writhing; coughing as fog caught their two throats or perhaps it was smoke from those below who had put on cigarettes or pipes, because tobacco smoke was coming up in drifts; leaning out then, so secure, from their window up above and left by their argument on terms of companionship unalloyed, Julia and Max could not but feel infinitely remote, although at the same time Julia could not fail to be remotely excited at themselves.

[*Party Going*, p. 150.]

This sentence, with its string of details held in suspension by the delayed appearance of the subject, with its parenthetical interruption between ". . . carpet or" and "with some kind . . . ," and with its difficult causal "through one part of . . ." (at first seen deceptively as parallel with the spatial "from above"), arrests forward movement and compels attention to pattern—Julia and Max vis à vis the crowd.

Another salient mannerism in *Party Going* is the use of demonstratives in place of articles. One instance in which this replacement has figurative value is Green's description of

[16] Discussing parataxis and hypotaxis, Eduard Norden takes a different position. He asserts that Vergil's frequent substitutions of a clause connected with the main statement merely by *et* or *que* for a clause that normally would be introduced by a subordinator (like *cum* or *simul*) reflect a desire to implicate the clause more closely in time with the main clause (*P. Vergilius Maro Aeneis Buch VI*, pp. 368–80).

Miss Fellowes's delirium, "And then when she thought she must be overwhelmed, or break, this storm would go back and those waters and her blood recede, that moon would go out above her head, and a sweet tide washed down from scalp to toes and she could rest" (p. 76). Since no moon has previously been mentioned in this passage, "that" points to a context for "moon" preceding the passage. It is "that moon" which presides over such delirium, and "that moon" is later identified when Edwards, in response to Thomson's lust, says, "You want the moon" (p. 203).

In view of Stokes's fine survey of the general stylistic peculiarities of Green's work and of the characteristics of particular novels, I have chosen in this chapter to concentrate on the kinds of interest in English prose Green showed in his second book and to indicate the ways in which he learned to control the stylistic devices in that book. Because of its size and because of its lack of the formal parameters characterizing verse, the novel cannot foreground language as pervasively as verse does (*pace* Joyce). One suspects, for example, that the inverted fifth foot of Wallace Stevens's line, "It can never be satisfied, the mind, never," is significant because it is one of only two inverted fifth feet in the poem. The first of these inverted feet is "even," which is almost a palindrome for "never." The linguistic economy of the novel is obviously much different, since the novel's size and its lack of equivalent positions encourage progressive movement. In *Living* and in the books that follow, however, Green developed ad hoc conventions for making the articulating process audible (or visible). From using ellipses and distortion of word order pervasively (though not consistently) in *Living*, Green learned to use these devices as responses to stress in *Party Going*.

IV
Discursive Figures

In Chapter II we discussed the norm of the traditional novel in terms of a strong linear or temporal push, a univocal anecdote, and a relative lack of self-reflectiveness, and the forms deviation from that norm has taken. Jakobson talks about the norms of poetry and realistic prose in terms of "metaphoric and metonymic poles":

> In poetry there are various motives which determine the choice between these alternants. The primacy of the metaphoric process in the literary school of romanticism and symbolism has been repeatedly acknowledged, but it is still insufficiently realized that it is the predominance of metonymy which underlies and actually predetermines the so-called "realistic" trend, which belongs to an intermediary stage between the decline of romanticism and the rise of symbolism and is opposed to both. Following the path of contiguous relationships, the realistic author metonymically digresses from the plot to the atmosphere and from the characters to the setting in space and time. He is fond of synecdochic details. In the scene of Anna Karenina's suicide Tolstoy's artistic attention is focused on the heroine's handbag; and in *War and Peace* the synecdoches "hair on the upper lip" or "bare shoulders" are used by the same writer to stand for the female characters to whom these features belong.[1]

[1] Roman Jacobson and Morris Halle, *Fundamentals of Language*, pp. 77–78.

The "realistic trend" is still normative for fiction in general and for English fiction in particular. It is Robbe-Grillet's contention in *For a New Novel* that despite the dislocations brought about by Proust, Joyce, Faulkner, Beckett, and others, the realistic or bourgeois novel is still a powerful norm against which the writer of the "new" novel must relentlessly rebel. David Lodge discusses this conflict in terms of "contemporaries" (Steiner's "daylight" or public writers, who assume a kind of *sensus communus*) and "moderns" (explorers of language and subjectivity, who assume an ambiguity in human experience).[2] I am less interested in the differences between Green and other "modern" novelists like Joyce, Beckett, and Robbe-Grillet than in those self-reflexive devices common to them all. Of the devices that we shall consider, rhyming is a mode of relating fictional elements; bound and compositional motifs are the elements related; enjambment is a device for violating the organizational commitments of the paragraph; the chapter is an architectural commitment comparable perhaps to the poetic line or the poetic stanza; and the agrammatical use of tense is a device for internal distancing rather than temporal shifting. These devices will now be examined in detail.

The term "rhyming" is taken from Jean Ricardou, who points out that, whereas film renders an instantaneous perception of diverse qualities or objects, the successive arrangement of literary signs necessarily entails limiting the number of objects or the complexity of a single object in a description. Because of their essential rarity, the objects described in the novel gain an increased significance, which increases the intensity of their relations and disposes them "to rhyme." Furthermore, the qualities of a literary object tend to generate other objects which incarnate the same or similar qualities.[3] Rhyming is consequently a literary phenomenon—one which

[2] David Lodge, *Language of Fiction*, pp. 244–45.
[3] Jean Ricardou, *Problèmes du nouveau roman*, pp. 70–72.

is peculiar to the relations between words—rather than a mimetic phenomenon—one which relates to the mimetic responsibility most writers have expressed vis-à-vis life. This distinction is made by Green in his comparison of painting and fiction (quoted in Chapter I), where he claims that the painter does not see more color than does the normal person but develops a compositional sense that enables him to give his paintings a life of their own. It is this *internal* play of forces, apprehended without too much difficulty in criticism of painting or of poetry, which has eluded many critics of the novel.

The phenomenon of rhyming, therefore, is generated by the mind's ambition for order, for pattern, for poetic justice. It is a symptom of the fact that the perceptual whole is always less than the sum of its parts. That is, in making sense of our experience we define the whole in terms of only some of its parts. This is true at a primary level of articulation—perception—and is reinforced at a secondary level of articulation—writing. In writing, what is lost in reference (the limitation of objects or of their complexity that Ricardou notes) is gained in sense. This *découpage,* which characterizes man as an animal that labors for sense, has its formal and most arbitrary representation in the line ending of a poem. Semantic *découpage,* of which metonymy and metaphor are examples, is a lesser mode of arbitrariness.

Dickens, for example, having to contend with the disruptions of continuity entailed by serial publication, uses the salient qualities of a character to generate ad infinitum settings, situations, and facts that evince those qualities. In this way metonymy is transformed into metaphor, contiguity into equivalence.

To one extent or another this process takes place in all novels, and it works against their horizontal thrust. In *Hard Times,* for example, Dickens shifted the axis as follows:

from Gradgrind's character, appearance, ideas, children, house, etc.

to Authoritarian rigidity and abstractness (rubric):
character
appearance
ideas
school
children
house
etc.

Before I illustrate how this rhyming process works in Green's novels, I should like to discuss the notions of bound and compositional motifs, which are the elements that enter into the rhyming mode. These notions are derived from Boris Tomashevsky's "Thematics," although I have reduced his more elaborate scheme to two notions and have changed his terminology.

Tomashevsky defines a motif as "the theme of an irreducible part of a work . . . each sentence, in fact, has its own motif," which may be a molecule of action, a character trait, or a descriptive detail. He then distinguishes between "bound motifs" and "free motifs": "Usually there are different kinds of motifs within a work. By simply retelling the story we immediately discover what may be *omitted* without destroying the coherence of the narrative and what may not be omitted without destroying the connections among events. The motifs which cannot be omitted are *bound motifs;* those which may be omitted without disturbing the whole causal-chronological course of events are *free motifs.*"[4] What Tomashevsky refers to as "free motifs" I refer to as "compositional motifs," since I wish to emphasize their special function in shaping our consciousness of events rather than their lack of causal responsibility. Moreover, it is not always possible to assign a motif to one of these two categories. For exam-

[4] Boris Tomashevsky, "Thematics," pp. 67–68. The italics are Tomashevsky's.

ple, the lawsuit in *Bleak House,* without which the story cannot proceed, is a clear example of a bound motif. The fog in that same book, which has symbolic import as well as descriptive interest but is not necessary to the progress of the story, is a clear example of a free motif. The fog in *Party Going,* however, seems to be a bound motif in the sense that it requires the party-goers to remain in the station hotel and engage in the combinations and permutations of relationships which that confinement entails, but the power of the motif is unaccounted for by that function. The fog motif is expressive of epistemological difficulty on the one hand and death on the other, and this compositional function (similar to Wallace Stevens's jar in Tennessee which gave composition to the landscape though "It did not give of bird or bush, / Like nothing else in Tennessee") is far more important than its function in the cause and effect nexus we presuppose as a working model of reality.

Bound and compositional motifs are analogous to kinds of evidence given in a jury trial. It is common in jury trials for an attorney to elicit information or judgments from a witness that are subsequently challenged by the opposing attorney as being irrelevant or immaterial—whether the testimony is based on hearsay, or based on materials not in evidence, or concerned with persons or issues not technically relevant to the trial. Although the jury is instructed to disregard such testimony, its inability to do so helps shape its decision. The bound motif is admissible evidence, whereas the compositional motif is inadmissible evidence that we hear anyway. That inadmissible evidence replenishes the store of possibilities Valéry wanted to see presented at any moment in the novel. Within the emotional economy of *Party Going,* Miss Fellowes dies a number of times, although in realistic terms she does not die. The frequent anticipations and evocations of her death establish the compositional, if not the chronological, fact of that event. That compositional death, in turn, reinvokes the actual death of the pigeon which begins the book. At the end of *Loving,* the compositional fact of Raunce's death is evoked by his cry "Edie," made in the exact tone with which the dying Mr. Eldon cried out "Ellen." In actual fact Raunce leaves for England with Edie, where they live "happily ever after." The central compositional fact of *Concluding* is the death of a young girl even though the chronological fact of that death is never established and even though the girl's fate has been shrouded in mystery.

As we have suggested, the elements entering into the rhyming mode need not be static; they may themselves be modes of action or kinds of relationships. It is important, moreover, to distinguish between the grammatical status of the motif (whether it is a thing, a relationship, or an action) and its effect on the reader. Regardless of their grammatical status, some motifs will have a more dynamic effect on the reader than others because of the work done by the rhyming process, just as the Miltonic simile, generating what Geoffrey Hartman calls "counterplots," will be much more dynamic than the simple analogy.[5] To illustrate these discursive figures, this inadmissible evidence, let us further consider the ways in which compositional motifs are used in Green's novels, and especially in *Concluding*.

Opposing the phenomenon Harry Stack Sullivan calls "selective inattention," Shklovsky's definition of art as "defamiliarization" or "dehabituation" is an attempt to describe its systematic way of renewing our awareness, of compelling us to confront qualities of our experience that have been screened out by the socialization process. Defamiliarization, then, is a systematic correction of selective inattention. One of Henry Green's frequent ploys is to use motifs of sensory deprivation or verbal inadequacy in order to defamiliarize interpersonal relationships and relations between characters and their environment.[6] The peculiar effect of this strategy is to intensify our sense of human separateness. Green's notions of non-

[5] See Geoffrey Hartman, "Milton's Counterplot."

[6] In the next chapter, we shall note other kinds of loss or deficiency that are signals for a problematic participation in one's environment. The protagonists of *Caught* and *Back* suffer an erotic loss that condenses

representational fiction and of obliquity are very close to what Shklovsky means by defamiliarization, just as the mimetic problems he points to underline the tenuous quality of personal communication (as opposed to the standardized communication of journalism). The strategy, therefore, behind Green's use of the motifs that we are examining is as follows: Green is aware of the disparity between the generic quality of words and the peculiar refractions of individual experience. This awareness makes him cautious about the possibility of direct personal communication. His own deafness and blindness becomes analogues in his novels for the separateness that must be overcome in human relationships and in the individual's apprehension of his environment. The artist's awareness, however, of these limitations forces him into a more self-conscious use of his artistic medium (in the painter's case, colors; in the novelist's case, words) to attain a "new level of communication." Green's earlier point about the number of painters who have poor eyesight resembles Edmund Wilson's notion of a wound that characterizes artists —the effort to overcome the deficiency generating extraordinary modes of communication.[7]

In *Blindness* the loss of sight means a loss of security for John Haye, an undermining of the relations between self and environment: "Everything was abstract now, personality had gone" (p. 93). In *Concluding* characters primarily are

---

the generalized sense of loss they feel as a result of war. The protagonist of *Back,* moreover, loses his leg during the war; the protagonist of *Caught* is hard of hearing. A number of Green's characters suffer from indigestion, one develops diabetes, and still another is gradually eroded by operations during the course of the novel.

[7] As analogues for human separateness, note the metaphorical equivalence of seeing and hearing in the following phrases from *Concluding:* there is a "megaphone of light" (p. 21); there is a "blinding silence" (p. 203); the sunlight "shone so loud" (p. 21); and the fog bank makes "all daylight deaf beneath" (p. 3). The last phrase resembles a lovely passage in the *Inferno,* Canto I: "And such as is he who gains willingly, and the time arrives which makes him lose, so that in all his thoughts he laments and is sad, such did the beast without peace make me, which, coming on against me, was pushing me back, little by little, thither where the Sun is silent." See Dante Alighieri, *The Divine Comedy,* p. 4.

blinded not *to* light but *by* light—by sunlight. An incident in *Pack My Bag* reveals Green's attitude toward sunlight. A young man is persecuted by some girls at a Hunt Ball because he complimented one of them, and Green comments, "It must be a question of the sun" (p. 227). In *Blindness,* Joan, who is bursting with sexual vitality, thinks, "She loved the sun, he took hold of you and drew you out of yourself so that you couldn't think, you just gave yourself up" (p. 132). The frequent blinding or dazzling by sunlight in *Concluding* is then expressive of the bombardment of personality by the sheer energy of life as it is manifested in both light and heat. It is a result of plenitude, as opposed to the deprivation in *Blindness.*[8]

When Mr. Rock enters Mrs. Blaine's kitchen, he is isolated from the girls by the "loud" sunlight that bisects the kitchen: "They were no more to him than light blue shadows" (p. 21). He is susceptible, however, to an intuition of "female curiosity" behind the cone of light in which he sits, which is like the "smell of a fox that has just slunk by, back of some bushes" (p. 24). He is also susceptible to his general bodily impressions: "And in a moment the old and famous man was left alone at table, altogether blinded by increasing brightness, before an empty plate and a cup that was warm, behind a rumbling stomach, left to dread the journey back with full buckets" (p. 29). This coenesthesis occurs in a later scene where Elizabeth and Sebastian, arms about each other, stop in the sunlight, which "was a load, a great cloak to clothe them, like a depth of warm water that turned the man's brown city outfit to a drowned man's clothes, the sun was so heavy, so encompassing betimes" (p. 55). In another scene Miss Edge and Miss Baker, sitting in a room partitioned into three parts by the sun, are separated in shadow, separated by a wedge of sunlight. Miss Edge pushes some

[8] The exceptions are Miss Baker's "sightless condition," a result of her sentimentality; Miss Marchbanks's "blinding headache," a result of her repression; and Miss Edge's "culpable blindness," one way of viewing her repressiveness.

azaleas into shadow before attempting to work out some solution to the disappearance of the two girls. Miss Baker, perplexed by this attempted explanation, "in perplexity turned toward Miss Edge, and was blinded by the sun" (pp. 164–67).

The most striking use of this motif is Miss Marchbanks's interrogation of Merode, whom she places where the sunlight in the room will dazzle her. For Merode, however, the sunlight is protection against the mechanical insistence of Miss Marchbanks's interrogation. Later in the scene, as Miss Marchbanks tries to elicit the facts of her escapade, Merode is no longer "blinded in sunlight, her eyes had caught on one of the black squares, as that pyjama leg had earlier been hooked on a briar" (p. 69). The black and white squares of a dado, as we shall see, counteract the chromaticism of the book, the former being an abstract reduction of the latter. As Miss Marchbanks keeps questioning Merode about her experience (the erotic nature of which is intimated by the pajama leg caught in the briar), Merode begins to sicken (as Miss Fellowes does in a less well-defined situation in *Party Going*). She is no longer dazzled by sunlight during the interrogation but "mesmerized by the black and white receding pavements" (p. 69).

Deafness, aphasia, and mimicry are more univocal analogues in this book for the separateness of human personality (mimicry coming under the heading of "verbal inadequacy" because it is an avoidance of communication). Mr. Rock's deafness is a source of continual misunderstandings, some of which are hilarious, as when Mr. Rock mistakes Mr. Adams's "you and your sort" for "lose the fort" and Adams tops him with "booze the port." Some of these misunderstandings reveal private meanings, as when Mr. Rock mistakes "you mean the weather" for "end of her tether" in relation to the missing girl. At least one of these misunderstandings is disturbing: Mr. Rock is not sure to whom the police sergeant is referring when he asks, "Now she's not disappeared, I hope, sir?" The police sergeant is referring to Rock's goose, but Mr. Rock is not sure he is not referring to the missing girl.

He echoes, "Disappeared? I know nothing" (p. 151). But Mr. Rock does know something, as does George Adams, the woodman, and in that sense they are implicated in the girls' disappearance. They both understand the unnatural strain to which the girls in school are subjected, and this implication in the girls' situation explains subtle, seemingly gratuitous expressions of guilt or defensiveness. For some reason Adams is relieved at the beginning of the book "to hear just a girl hollering" (pp. 10–11). Later he becomes somewhat paranoid after he has been questioned by Miss Baker. Mr. Rock is "horrified" at the disappearance of the two girls when he hears about it; later he notices "with a dreadful reluctance" that the uppermost pedal of the policeman's bicycle still turns (p. 74). The bicycle subsequently becomes associated with sexual release: As Miss Edge commits herself to proposing to Mr. Rock, she feels "as though on top of a hill in a dream on a bicycle with no brakes" (p. 241). Despite their awareness of the stress which the system has exerted on the girls, Rock and Adams are both isolated by their egotism, by their efforts to keep what is theirs. Mr. Rock's deafness is one of a constellation of traits having to do with old age and impending death—the most isolating of facts.

Elizabeth's aphasia and Sebastian's mimicry are also analogues for separateness. The only time Elizabeth can talk coherently or Sebastian can sustain his own voice is when they are alone together. Sexual fulfillment, like the sun in which they "drown," brings them out. Even together, however, and always with other people, their self-assertion can break down under stress. Sebastian uses a false "bantering tone with which to speak of his profession" in response to Elizabeth's scrutiny of their relationship (p. 44). Later in the book Sebastian assumes his lecturer's voice in an attempt to subdue Elizabeth's efforts at self-revelation. In that scene Elizabeth becomes incoherent in trying to express the relation between humans and animals in terms of the inscrutability of their motives. Not only is she incoherent in this discussion, but she incorrectly assumes that the people around her know the real subject of the discussion—which is Mr. Rock's cottage (pp. 206–9).

Just as the motifs of sensory deprivation in Green's books slide subtly from their function as analogues of human separateness to formal means of defamiliarization, so the motif of mimicry slides from its representational function to a formal function. In *Party Going,* for example, the central deficiency of the party-goers (associated with the illness of Miss Fellowes) is a lack of fellow feeling. Green guards against sentimentalizing this norm: An unidentified man keeps making gratuitous appearances, somewhat like the Cheshire cat in *Alice's Adventures in Wonderland.* First appearing as a "rough looking customer" who commiserates with Miss Fellowes on the bad service at the bar, he is later seen watching her and winking each time he looks away. He later follows her as she is carried into the hotel, and he assumes a variety of accents with Alex, who thinks he may be the house detective. He is later described as looking like an escaped prisoner. Still later, having been used by Robert to get a message through to Thomson (Julia's chauffeur), he is described as someone who has "always interfered." He comes into contact with all the characters in the book and is in transit between lower and upper classes, by both his changing accent and his actual mobility. He represents a kind of parodic fellow feeling, funny because it is so gratuitous. Green is very careful not to sentimentalize the communal feeling among the masses below; at the same time he establishes such a feeling as a norm for the book. The protean stranger (appearing at first as a threatening house detective because he is in some way to find the party-goers out) is a parody of the central value in the book.

Mimicry or echoing is also a formal or literary quality of *Concluding,* as well as a quality of life which it represents or re-creates. The constant mimicry in this book is one aspect of its multiplying resonances. Besides the constant mimicry of characters (Sebastian mimics particular people and roles constantly, the girls imitate Sebastian and Miss Marchbanks, and Rock mimics Miss Edge), there are also false echoings of what has been said or done, which lead to all kinds of false rumors and red herrings. There is also a mysterious echo, the acoustics of which are under dispute in the book. This dispute over acoustics makes the source of the cry "Mar-ee, Mar-ee" problematic. When Merode's aunt, echoing Miss Marchbanks (although neither she nor the two principals are aware of this fact), suggested sleepwalking as an explanation of the two girls' disappearance, "Miss Baker was so flabbergasted at this forgotten echo of the dawn that, without more ado, she took the woman up to Merode at once" (p. 135). Again the source of this echo is not clear since the principals have not mentioned or heard the suggestion of sleepwalking before. The form of the book is that of a series of ripples from a central disturbance which remains obscure although intimated.

In discussing blindness, we touched briefly on motifs of light and color, which are always conspicuous in Green's work. We can initiate our discussion of these motifs by recalling Shelley's ambivalent lines from *Adonais:*

> Life, like a dome of many-colored glass,
> Stains the white radiance of Eternity,
> Until Death tramples it to fragments.
>
> [ll. 462–64]

At the opening of *Concluding,* Mr. Rock is described as coming out of the fog: "His white head was gray, and white the reflected torch light on the thick spectacles he wore" (p. 5). The inversion of the second clause, with "white" shifted from an epithet to an attribute,[9] foregrounds the word "white."

[9] Jean Cohen, *Structure du langage poétique,* p. 141. An epithet applies only to part of the extension of a noun and, if used grammatically, occurs in this form: the *red* balloon, where it limits the noun. An attribute applies to the entire extension of a noun and, if used grammatically, occurs in this form: the elephant is *wrinkled,* where it does not limit the noun.

Mr. Rock's three animals are white, and Mr. Rock observes that Ted (the goose) and Daisy (the pig) might be mistaken for each other at a distance because of this common trait. A suggestion of Shelley's "white radiance" comes when the sun makes the goose "a blaze of white" (p. 72). During the last scenes of the book, Mr. Rock's thoughts are on death. Descending the terraces from the mansion, "He cautiously lifted boots one after the other in an attempt to avoid cold lit veins of quartz in flagstones underfoot because they appeared to him like sunlight that catches in sharp glass beneath an incoming tide, where the ocean foams ringing an Atlantic" (p. 245). This white light, which in Shelley's metaphor precedes and survives the refractions of life's prism, is the whiteness of death. (We shall soon note that whiteness also associates the animals metonymically with the girls.) In *Concluding* one has a white "meta-light," which is refracted by life into the chromatic. As opposed to the radiance of eternity, motifs of sunlight, moonlight, and artificial light evoke varying forms of vital energy or varying apprehensions of it.[10]

As I indicated in the discussion of blindness, sunlight is identified with vitality and growth, Mr. Rock's old age being expressed by Mrs. Beame's ambiguous statement, "You're one who's never in the light . . ." (p. 26). The sun generates and reveals primal energy. When Sebastian finds one of the missing girls, her knee is described as "A knee which, brilliantly polished over bone beneath, shone in the sort of pool she had made for herself in the fallen world of birds, burned there like a piece of tusk burnished by shifting sands, or else a wheel revolving at such speed that it had no edges and was white, thus communicating life to ivory, a heart to the still, and the sensation of a crash to this girl who lay quiet, reposed" (p. 56). The sunlight also reveals the submarine life of the impulses:

[10] In the above quotation, the "cold lit veins of quartz" and the "sunlight that catches in sharp glass beneath an incoming tide" seem otherworldly, dead. This passage differs sharply from the descriptions of brilliant, warm sunlight that pervade the book.

a redhead caught fire with sun like a flare and, out of the sun, eyes, opening to reflected light, like jewels enclosed by flesh coloured anemones beneath green clear water when these yawn after shrimps, disclosed great innocence in a scene on which no innocence had ever shone, where life and pursuit was fierce, as these girls came back to consciousness from the truce of a summer after luncheon before the business of the dance.

[P. 109.]

At one point in the book, sunlight is specifically associated with sexuality: In a conversation Mr. Rock cannot follow, Mrs. Baines and the girls associate sunlight with pregnancy (pp. 26–27). Insofar as sunlight is associated with eroticism, it is associated with a healthy eroticism.

Moonlight, on the other hand, is associated with the uncanny and the forbidden. The sexuality it is seen to represent is a warped sexuality. In *Caught,* Pye, who becomes a kind of "Pierrot lunaire" in the book, acts out his torment, a false recollection of incest, compulsively, in moonlight. In *Concluding,* Mr. Rock and Elizabeth go at night to a "ball," where all sorts of uncanny things happen. By the light of the moon ("a huge female disc"), Mr. Rock enters the shade of the "enormous, over-hanging portals" and is lost there "as if by magic." Elizabeth then sees his "dead hand come forth to stab the bell a second time" (p. 190). After this descent into Hades and partial emergence, a magical or fairy tale sequence of events follows: Mr. Rock's eyes are "lensed eyes" (he wears glasses, but the phrase suggests a snake); Liz gives a "gasp of disenchantment"; Mrs. Blain says of Mary that "she might've given [her] a ring" (involving a pun on "ring" in this context); the staff do not hear the "cold hum of violins in sharp, moonstruck window glass," and as they hurried closer to the dance, "the whole edifice began to turn, even wooden pins which held the panelling noiselessly revolved to the greater, ever greater sound"; Mr. Rock is led down into a strange, subterranean lair where he finds initiation rites, "ancient music," and a "rajah's treasure of Moira's eyes";

having emerged from his ordeal and told his daughter that the girls are fiends, Mr. Rock enters Miss Edge's study, where she is smoking a "weed," holding it like a wand; Mr. Rock has to descend a cliff, moving backward (like a crab) in a metaphorical ocean; the mysterious cry of "Mar-ee" occurs three times; the goose, Ted, flies for the first time, and the other two animals come home, the pig, Daisy, with a satin slipper around her neck. These uncanny goings-on, this moonlit world, suggest the repressed and forbidden preconscious: When gods are banished, they go underground and become fairies. Green almost never engages in psychological analysis, in direct psychological probing; instead, by means of the repetitions and associations of compositional motifs, he suggests the preconscious life which underlies personality, as well as the warping of that life.

Caught provides more dramatic examples of "stained" or artificial light and colors. In that book we are alerted very early to the evocative power of colors and of filtered and reflected light: "It was disastrous that the woman who took the boy away should be his Fireman Instructor's sister. Hardly less fatal that the store had been lit by stained glass windows in front of arc lamps which cast the violent colours of that glass over the goods laid out on counters" (p. 11). One understands immediately why the first statement is true, but why are those violent colors so fatal? Green elaborates: "For both it was the deep colour spilled over these objects that, by evoking memories they would not name, and which they could not place, held them, and then led both to a loch-deep unconsciousness of all else" (p. 12). What is fatal about these colors is the circuit they create between the personality and the preconscious. As I have pointed out, Green does not plumb the inner life, but he realizes surfaces which often suggest the common springs of personality.

Early in the book Richard Roe recalls the store in which his son Christopher was kidnapped. It is lit by stained-glass windows, which flood it with color, and by neon light. The predominant color in the trading scenes that the windows depict is blue, which is associated with a kind of Aegean sea of the imagination. It is later a property of moonlight, which is often associated with fantasy. In an early episode violet and yellow are associated with a kind of death wish. The store having reminded Richard of the fire station, which in turn reminds him of an abbey that he visited as a child, he remembers being taken around a ledge just below the windows of the abbey and experiencing the "terror of the urge to leap." His back is to "deep violet and yellow Bible stories on the glass" (p. 11). The colors reflected on the flagstones are the colors his blood seems to have turned. Later in the book Pye has a dream about the mental hospital where his sister is a patient, in which bars cast over him a "zebra light," and "dry, striped men with yellow surgeon's dress asked about his business" (p. 85). Pink and red, the most disturbing colors in the book, are associated with both war and sex. The reflected light on the sidewalks, which transforms London during the bombardment, is pink. Inside the store where Christopher is kidnapped by Pye's frustrated sister, neon lights shed a pink glow that mixes with the other color tones. Women's nails as well as toy fire engines are red. Richard Roe meditates at one point that it would have been better to paint the real engines "pink, a boudoir shade, to match that half light which was to settle, night after night, around the larger conflagrations" (p. 149). The reflection of lamps in an intimate nightclub is coral. Violet, as I have pointed out, is initially associated with the death impulse; it is later, as a mixture of red and blue, associated with various kinds of intimacy. A gentian bulb lights the basement in which the firemen race cockroaches. Richard Roe recalls this light while sitting in a similar light in a nightclub, listening to the "blues" (which are usually pictured as indigo) (pp. 111–12). Green is associated with initiation: The firemen are "green" at their first fire, and the heavens turn green for a moment outside the perimeter of the glow shed by the fire (pp. 181–82).

It is also associated with decadence: Prudence, the young woman whose favors Pye shares and pays for, is dressed in green, the color of a cod's head that a kitten swipes at in the gutter (p. 64).

I do not wish to distort the book by making the use of these colors overschematic or by forgetting that they are objective, descriptive elements, but the peculiar "fatality" of the colors in the kidnapping episode and the insistent foregrounding of these colors during crucial scenes seem to give them a figurative function. However schematic or unschematic their use, colors (and especially light-dyes) establish circuits with the wellsprings of feeling. Green's novels are sometimes like fictive spectroscopes that generate spectra in accordance with affective principles.[11]

The rich chromaticism of *Concluding,* the prism of colors Miss Edge admires through the frame of her window (p. 15), is contrasted with the black and white perspective of the dado:

> The panelling was remarkable in that it boasted a dado designed to continue the black and white tiled floor in perspective, as though to lower the ceiling. But Miss Edge had found marble tiles too cold to her toes, had had the stone covered in parquet blocks, on which were spread State imitation Chinese Kidderminster rugs. As a result, the receding vista of white and black lozenges set from the rugs to four feet up the walls, in precise and radiating perspective, seemed altogether out of place next British dragons in green and yellow; while the gay panelling above, shallow carved, was genuine, the work of a master, giving Cupid over and over in a thousand poses, a shock, a sad surprise in such a room.
>
> [PP. 11–12.]

This description is an abstract design of the entire book. As we have seen, Merode, who has been found in a dazzling "fallen world of birds," sickens on the black and white loz-

[11] This characteristic links Green with Wallace Stevens, whose "harmonium" of colors humanizes the world that he perceives.

enges of the dado, an awareness of which accompanies Miss Marchbanks's interrogation of the girl. The effect of the switch from dazzling sunlight to the black and white dado is like that of a science-fiction film, in which a scientist develops and uses a chemical which gives him X-ray vision. That visual alteration turns the world into a wasteland, a jumble of skeletons. The clearest contrast between the chromatic and the black and white pattern occurs at lunch, where Miss Winstanley (who is in love with Sebastian) suggests that the school get Chinese pheasants for the grounds. The red and gold plumage of these birds contrasts with Miss Baker's recollection of a "black and white farm" where she was brought up. Later on, Miss Edge, wondering what to do about a directive she has received to begin a pig farm, says of Miss Baker, "her colleague would just remark . . . 'how quaint, how black and white' " (p. 125). It is interesting that Miss Edge, who is hated by the major characters in the book is yet better able to appreciate, if not to participate in, the variegated richness of life than is the sentimental Miss Baker.

Other compositional motifs generating underplots in the book relate to flowers and animals. In *Concluding* these motifs tend to work in a more analogical fashion than do the motifs of light and color, though the analogies always remain more like the Miltonic simile than like the illustrative simile or metaphor. Flowers, for example, are associated on the one hand with the girls, who carry red and white flowers and gold azaleas (p. 58). The first two colors have been associated with Merode, whose hair and pajamas are red and whose face is white (her "red hair was streaked across a white face" [p. 56]); the gold of the azaleas has been associated both with Marion, whose hair is golden, and with Moira, whose legs have a gold haze. A mass of bloom is later described as being "almost the color of Merode's hair in her bath" (p. 95), and Merode is described as a water lily. Once these associations are established, the poignancy of the girls' inevitable aging can be expressed at the dance by means of these blooms:

A white bunch of children, stood in the doorway, fell open to let him through like a huge dropped flower losing petals on a path.
[P. 230.]

. . . and a second time that group of children opened, reclosed behind the couple trailing after, having parted as another vast bloom might that, torn by a wind in summer, lies collectedly dying on crushed fallen leaves, to be divided by one and then two walkers, only for a strain of wind to reassemble it, to be rolled back complete on the path once more, at the whim of autumnal airs again.
[P. 231.]

On the other hand, flowers are also associated with intuitions of sexual disturbance. As Miss Baker and Miss Edge return to the estate, Miss Edge scans the "eunuch scentless flowers" lining the road for Merode and Mary (p. 75). Later Miss Edge, suspecting that the girls in the lunch hall are sharing a secret relating to the gathered masses of flowers, becomes "deathly hot" and concludes that a corpse is beneath the flowers. In small talk Miss Winstanley points out that azaleas can bring on hay fever, "'And pine branches asthma,' Edge said, rather wild, not yet herself quite" (p. 104). Within this context these disorders take on the aspect of psychosomatic manifestations of repression. Contrasted with the traditional azaleas and rhododendrons, with which the school has always been decorated on special occasions, are the fir trees covered with salt, which Miss Marchbanks prefers as decorations. (Later in the book the moon is described as "now all powerful, it covered everything with salt, and bewigged distant trees" [p. 189]. As we recall, that moon has also been described as a "huge female disc.")

Animal imagery pervades the figures of speech. In Mrs. Baine's kitchen feminine curiosity is described as like the "smell of a fox that has just slunk by, back of some bushes" (p. 24). This motif (unlike Lawrence's fox) is associated with feminine vitality. At one point, after Miss Baker has heard the hidden, naked Elizabeth laugh at her, she is described as "a hen, watching behind for a fox" (p. 154). Hens are unfortunate animals in Green's books. In *Blindness* "a hen was taken with asthma over her newly-laid" (p. 98). Joan has a "crazy hen" in the disused conservatory: "She was crazy because she would cry aloud for hours on end and Joan never knew why, though perhaps it was for a chick that a fox had carried off once" (p. 134). This conflict between hen and fox is clearly a suggestive one for Green and takes on significance from its context.

Mr. Rock's animals seem to express different modes of sexuality: his goose, Ted, becomes associated with sexual power. The enigmas of *Concluding* are summed up in the following riddle, which Miss Edge and Miss Baker try to unravel: "Who is there furnicates [*sic*] besides his goose?" Actually, they are not even sure whether this is an accurate version of the riddle, which they received in the mail. At lunch Miss Edge complains about the danger the goose represents: "A blow from one of its great wings . . . one blow, in one of its savage tempers, and the miserable bird could smash a leg" (p. 106). Although the lovesick Miss Winstanley tries to point out that this description of Ted's power and potential destructiveness is more appropriate to swans than to geese, Miss Edge's assertion recalls the deceptive description of Merode when she is found: Her "red hair was streaked across a white face and matted by salt tears, who was in pyjamas and had one leg torn to the knee" (p. 56). The coordinating "and" makes it appear as if Merode's leg, not her pajama leg, is torn to the knee: Later, when Miss Edge tells Merode's aunt that Merode "has torn the leg," the aunt replies, "But you told me she was not hurt" (p. 130). Ted is then connected with the compositional, if not actual, fact of an injury Merode has suffered the previous night. Merode has been found in a "fallen world of birds" (p. 56). The sexual connection becomes clear if we recall that the repressed Miss Marchbanks's ulcer is described as "a blood stained dove with tearing claws" (p. 41), and that Miss Marchbanks wants the senior girls to report deviant behavior "before the bird is flown, so to speak" (p. 50). Perhaps the climactic moment of the book is Ted's flight, which seems to be an explosion of all the tension that has accumulated throughout the book. Its timing seems appropriate in that the uncanny sequence of events which it climaxes relates at least in part to repressed or underground sexuality. Ted's flight is then parodied by the flight of a white slipper that has been mysteriously tied around Daisy's neck; it also takes off at the end: "He [Mr. Rock] hurled the shoe away. Once it was no longer in moonlight it disappeared, the thing might have flown" (p. 254).

Like Ted, Daisy and Alice (Mr. Rock's pig and cat respectively) are associated with the erotic life of the book. That they are identified with each other by color and by analogy (at the end Daisy follows "like a cat" in fits and starts) indicates that they are a sort of paradigm of this life. Note that a declension takes place twice in the novel: Mr. Rock thinks, "Elizabeth, Eliza, Liz" (p. 8); another trio of names, "Marion, Merode, Mary," occurs later. At one point Miss Baker confuses Mary with Merode (p. 131); at another point Miss Edge notes that a doll, which seems to be a miniature of Mary, "could be Merode or even Marion" (p. 131); later still Elizabeth is mistaken for Mary (p. 190). The impersonal uniformity of institutional life (all of the girls' names beginning with the letter "m") parallels and controverts the prepersonal, common springs of sexuality.

Whereas Ted is associated with aggresive power, Daisy, though also having traces of malevolence, is associated with an unselfconscious fleshiness. The "great pink mouth" is like the wet, pink mouths of the girls (pp. 60, 122). The pig is associated in particular with Elizabeth, who has been experiencing the pleasing lethargy of sexual satisfaction with Sebastian. At one point "the group around Daisy ceased to exclaim the better to watch the woman old enough to be its mother" —Elizabeth (p. 59). At another point Miss Baker is afraid that the sergeant might be referring to Elizabeth when he says, "He's got his sow along after all" (p. 151). Daisy's "golden fangs" remind us, however, of the fierce though innocent impulses we glimpsed in the dissolving view of the girls that begins the middle section of the book. Of similar quality is Elizabeth's expression of "satisfied guile" as she plans her evening with Sebastian (p. 36). One of Mr. Rock's most pressing concerns is to fight "swine fever," about which he talks to Sebastian, Moira, and Miss Edge. He wants to give a "brief weekly homily on the care of pigs" to the girls, after which, when they are older, one or more might be encouraged to "have a go at this filthy swine fever" (p. 194).

Alice, the cat, is associated with the enigmatic aspects of the erotic. She is related to Mary's doll, and Miss Marchbanks, in trying to find out what has happened to Mary and Merode, keeps referring to Alice as a kind of link in mysterious chain (p. 66). In our first view of the cat, she keeps "herself dry where every blade of grass bore its dark, mist laden strings of water" (p. 5).

In *Party Going* we noted that the fall of a bird disturbs us as we read the book, like the proverbial fallen sparrow. The movements of birds in that book, moreover, seem to signal a psychic condensation or sublimation. The fall of the bird that opens *Party Going* is like the condensation of the fog, whereas the flight of birds in that book is like its evaporation. We have noted that in *Concluding* birds function as expressions of libidinal energy. More generally, however, birds seem to signal an abundance of life. A cloud of starlings rising from the woods is concomitant with the girls' rising in their dormitories "with a sound of bees" (p. 19). In a few other scenes the girls, expectant or animated, are compared to birds. Later in the book, Mr. Rock witnesses the return home of swarms of starlings, swooping "through a thickening curve, in the enormous echo of blood, or of the sea" (p. 177). Mr. Rock, whose thoughts are on death through the last part of the book, says of the experience, "I'm glad I had that once more." The movement of birds is also a signal for the movement of time and for a shift in awareness. Birds rise at dawn, roost at noon, and settle at evening. The three sections of *Concluding* correspond to these movements (though the middle section takes place at teatime rather than at noon):

> A single pigeon, black in thickening sky, flew swift and on past the park.
>
> It was dusk.
>
> [P. 187.]

This progression, foregrounded by the fact that each sentence is a paragraph, is a progression of mood as well as of time.

One of the recurring animal motifs in Green's books is the trapped or dead mouse. In *Caught* Richard Roe and his son come across a dead mouse in the summer house. In *Back* Charley Summers says that in prison camp he kept a mouse in a cage that he had made. In *Loving* a mouse is trapped in the works of a weathervane. In *Concluding*, however, Green varies the motif: As Miss Edge opens curtains described as "red lilies over a deeper red," a "horrid bat" flies into the room. Miss Edge dives for a wicker basket containing the pieces of an anonymous letter that she received that morning, and when she rises and takes off the basket, a piece of paper with the word "furnicates" [*sic*] on it is caught in her hair (p. 12).

A story Miss Baker narrates leads us metonymically from the color motif to another salient motif or underplot in *Concluding:* that of Mary's doll. " 'Yet, you know, where I was brought up in the country, on a black and white farm,' she lied. . . . 'I was out to pick apples one day and the pigs were loose in the orchard. It was rather thundery weather, so I had my mackintosh, which I left below while I was up the ladder. But I suppose I must have been preoccupied, because they ate it, every scrap' " (p. 152). This mackintosh figures in another incident. At lunch Miss Edge suspects that Mary's corpse is to be found under the flowers which have been collected for decoration. Later on she discovers a "rabbity Rag Doll dressed gaily in miniature Institute pyjamas, painted with a grotesque caricature of Mary's features on its own flat face, laid disgustingly on a bit of mackintosh, embowered by these blooms" (p. 140). Still later Miss Edge accounts for her fainting at the sight of this doll by saying that she had thought it was a dead rabbit and that she has a "terror of rabbits dead" (p. 141). Although these passages are somewhat enigmatic, the collocation of details is suggestive. A doll that is a miniature version of Mary is discovered after flowers have been carried away; some notion of "deflowering" is suggested, with its resulting pregnancy. The doll is discovered on a piece of mackintosh, which in Miss Baker's story is eaten by pigs and is thus suggestive of the placenta. The doll is described as "rabbity," and Miss Edge says that she mistook it for a dead rabbit, of which she has a horror. Since rabbits are associated with procreation in common parlance, the inverted phrase "terror of rabbits dead," which foregrounds both of the inverted words, suggests abortion. Associations with *Alice's Adventures in Wonderland,* which has strong elements of birth trauma, also stipple this underplot. When Mr. Rock and Elizabeth are arguing whether or not to inform the supervisors about the missing girl, a rabbit is again alluded to: "Unseen, a rabbit, which had come out of its hole fifty feet away, stamped a hind leg back" (p. 172). Mary's doll is also associated with Alice, the cat. When Miss Marchbanks places the doll on Merode's lap, "This small weight woke the girl who, when she first opened eyes, saw what she dizzily took to be Alice, exactly as Miss Marchbanks had offered the animal curled up at rest" (p. 154). Moira's remark about Alice—"What mightn't Alice be able to tell?" (p. 50)—summarizes the displacements and condensations that account for the dream-like quality Mark Schorer assigns to the book.[12]

Ambiguities also characterize the ways in which drowning is alluded to in *Concluding,* as well as glimpses into depths.

[12] Mark Schorer, "The Real and Unreal Worlds of Henry Green," p. 5.

Sebastian and Elizabeth drown in sunlight, in sensual fulfillment. Their lovemaking, however, is rendered in grotesque marine imagery that makes us uncomfortable with their passion (p. 55). Later, as Mr. Rock descends into the girls' underground lair, putting "a foot forward as though about to enter an ocean" (p. 203), he becomes aware of the fiendish aspect that repressed, forbidden sexuality can take on. Referring to the girls as "fiends," he evokes the condition of gods who are driven underground.

During our discussion of light and color, we quoted a passage giving a dissolving view of the girls under the aspect of sunlight, a view of the submarine life of the impulses. The run-on sentence, generated by strings of participles, prepositions, and subordinators, becomes somewhat bewildering to follow and makes the relation between the innocence and fierceness of these girls problematic.[13] This scene undergoes what Ricardou calls an *éclatement:*[14] Elements of it recur separately in other scenes of the book. At the dance a girl chosen to dance "would give a little start, open those great eyes, much greater than jewels . . . " (p. 198). As a number of girls solicit Mr. Rock for a dance, he "could feel their moist fingers' skin, the tropic, anemone suction of soft palms on rheumatic, chalky knuckles" (p. 233). Suspicions about Mary having actually drowned are resonant with the instances of compositional drowning that I have cited: "Who could say what might be in that water" (p. 52). Finally, the drowning of Mr. Rock as he descends the terraces of the school on his way home is related to death. Later in his voyage home Mr. Rock, who is afraid of the dark, anticipates his walk through the beeches: "Then he recollected the black tide that was almost upon them. Indeed, raising eyes from a treacherous path, he saw

[13] If one compares Yeats's "murderous innocence of the sea" (an image of history in "A Prayer for My Daughter") with his "ceremony of innocence" (an image of civilization in "The Second Coming"), one sees a similar play on the notion of innocence.

[14] Ricardou, *Problèmes du nouveau roman,* p. 185.

the beeches like frozen milk, and frozen swimming-bath blue water, already motionless in a cascade, soundless from a height, not sixty yards in front" (p. 249). The pun on "beech" that the image of drowning generates connects this passage with the scene of Sebastian's and Elizabeth's lovemaking among the branches of a fallen beech. As in Lawrence, death and abundant life are alternative expressions of the erotic in this book.

Green's use of compositional motifs, then, creates a dissolving view of the events in the story, in which human actions and values give way to their preverbal, sensory equivalents. Perception or awareness never really begins and never really ends. In *Party Going* the characters are "party going" only in an anticipative sense; the "party going" in a progressive present sense is outside the chronological span of the book. In *Caught* Pye dreams about the mental institution to which his sister is confined and then pays an actual visit that has the same disturbing associations as his dream (such as an equivalence between the mental hospital and the fire brigade). Green's compositional motifs make us aware that though we may think the significant event is taking place before us, it is only about to, and the event dissolves into a multitude of affective and conative possibilities. These compositional motifs keep replenishing our sense of the possible, of the latent, much in the way Valéry prescribed. One of the best examples of how this dissolving view operates over the course of a whole work is G. K. Chesterton's *The Man Who Was Thursday*, where the ostensible plot of the book dissolves very gradually as we go along into the real plot.

In discussing character and plot in *Tom Jones*, Ian Watt concludes:

Tom Jones, then, would seem to exemplify a principle of considerable significance for the novel form in general: namely, that the importance of the plot is in inverse proportion to that of character. This principle has an interesting corollary: the organization of the narrative into an extended and complex formal structure will tend to turn the protagonists into its passive agents, but it will offer compensatingly greater opportunities for the introduction of a variety of minor characters, whose treatment will not be hampered in the same way by the roles which they are allotted by the complications of the narrative design.[15]

I should like to propose a comparable hypothesis: that the significance and power of free or compositional motifs vary in inverse proportion to the significance and power of bound motifs. The complaints usually expressed about Thomas Hardy concern the power and obtrusiveness of his bound motifs: the reappearances of the furmity woman and Newson in *The Mayor of Casterbridge;* the overheard conversations in the same novel; the chance meetings and failures to meet in *Tess of the D'Urbervilles* (including Tess's chance meeting with Alec after he has become a preacher, her failure to find Angel's parents at home, and Angel's failure to find Tess's note); and the role of Little Father Time in *Jude the Obscure.* (Hardy has frequently been praised for his free or compositional motifs: the Roman ruins in *The Mayor of Casterbridge;* Flintcome Ash, with its arctic birds and demonic thresher, in *Tess of the D'Urbervilles;* and Jude's catching cold the day he finally arrives at Christminster in *Jude the Obscure.*) One notes, on the other hand, that writers like Hammett and Laclos have been praised by the French structuralists for the intricacy of their bound motifs. A corollary of the above hypothesis is that the novelist whose work is characterized by many and/or powerful bound motifs is strongly deterministic in world view, whereas the novelist whose work is characterized by many and/or significant free or compositional motifs is strongly synchronistic in world view. The difference is that the determinist is attentive to the cause-and-effect relationships of events taking place serially, whereas the "synchronist" (if you will pardon the malapropism) is attentive to

[15] Ian Watt, *The Rise of the Novel,* p. 279.

meaningful relationships between events occurring at a given moment in time. Two examples of this synchronism are the view of Occasionalists that events in the outer (or objective) and inner (or subjective) worlds are parallel, this parallelism being guaranteed by God;[16] and the view implicit in the Chinese *Book of Changes* that all events taking place at a given moment are meaningfully related to one another, without God as a guarantor. Hardy is a determinist, with a strong sense, however, of the synchronistic relations of man and nature. Green is a synchronist who is not particularly impressed with the human legislation of events and who has no compelling notion of fate. In discussing the lyrical novel, Ralph Freedman points out the lyrical novelist's relation to time: "Facts and relations, rendered formless by the deceptive time sequences of the external world, are brought together in the artist's apprehension, in his 'rhythmical' or 'formal' recreation of life in abstract or 'symbolic' forms."[17] Compositional motifs, then, are contemporaneous in a poetic sense—in terms of an availability that is not earned by a narrative sequence.

More radical than rhyming is a discursive figure similar to enjambment in verse. Instead of violating the poetic line, it violates the integrity of the paragraph. In *Party Going* this enjambment is used to generate an extremely rapid montage that creates a metaphorical equivalence between neighboring elements. Frequently, the hinge for this montage is the pseudo-organizational "and": "Already both had been made to regret they had left such and such a dress behind and it was because he felt it impossible to leave things as they were with Angela . . . that Robin came back to apologize" (p. 29). This sentence moves from an account of Claire and Evelyn discussing their clothes to a completely disconnected (in a metonymic sense) account of Robin returning to find Angela. The "and" acts as an equal sign, equating two species of fatuousness. If we compare the sequence of paragraphs to the se-

[16] See Arnold Geulincx, *Annota ad Metaphysica*, pp. 296, 307.
[17] Ralph Freedman, *The Lyrical Novel*, p. 191.

quence of lines in a verse, the clause following "and" is a kind of *contrerejet*.[18] It violates the homogeneity of the paragraph and belongs metonymically with the following paragraph. The *écart* or deviation involved in this displacement must be resolved metaphorically.

Robbe-Grillet is rather expert at using the *contrerejet* in *The Voyeur:*

Mathias had no time to wait for what was going to happen next—supposing that anything was going to happen next. He was not even certain the moans came from this house; he had guessed they came from a source still closer, less muffled than they would have been by a closed window. In thinking it over he wondered if he had heard only moans, inarticulate sounds; had there been identifiable words? In any case it was impossible for him to remember what they were. Judging from the quality of her voice—which was pleasant, and not at all sad—the victim must have been a very young woman, or a child. She was standing against one of the iron pillars that supported the deck above; her hands were clasped behind the small of her back, her legs braced and slightly spread, her head leaning against the column. Her huge eyes inordinately wide (whereas all the passengers were squinting because the sun had begun to break through), she continued to look straight ahead of her, with the same calmness with which she had just now looked into his own eyes.[19]

The "she" in this passage is what Jean Cohen, following Jespersen, calls a "shifter" word, a word whose meaning varies with the situation.[20] It refers anaphorically to a girl being menaced in a scene that Mathias viewed on his way to the boat; it refers cataphorically, however, to a girl on the boat who is looking at Mathias. The menace connected with the

[18] With regard to enjambment, *rejet* occurs when most of the sentence is in the first line and only a segment is carried over to the next line. That segment is the *rejet*. *Contrerejet* occurs when most of the sentence is in the second line and only a segment has occurred in the first line. That segment is the *contrerejet*. These are common terms in French metrics.

[19] Alain Robbe-Grillet, *The Voyeur,* p. 20.

[20] Cohen, *Structure du langage poétique,* p. 157.

first girl is transferred to the second girl vis-à-vis Mathias, and that menace is transferred still further as the book goes on. We are never quite sure if any scene is "real" in the sense of being part of a nexus of events that we can call a story, or whether it is a latent possibility in the situation, a menace projected by Mathias's pathological obsession. In other words, at each moment we have the option of taking a scene as an event or as a digression.

Rejets as well as *contrerejets* occur in *The Voyeur:* "There was something missing from the drawing, although it was difficult to tell exactly what. Mathias decided that something was either not correctly drawn—or else missing altogether. Instead of the pencil, his right hand was holding the wad of cord he had just picked up from the deck. He looked at the group of passengers in front of him. . . . "[21] In this case the *rejet* connects the "something missing" from Mathias's drawing with the cord that he had picked up from the deck and that is connected with the menaced girl on ship. This "something missing" pullulates as the book goes on.

The following is an example of *rejet* in *Party Going:* "Alex came up and said what they saw now was like a view from the gibbet and she exclaimed against that. And Miss Fellowes wearily faced another tide of illness. Aching all over she watched helpless while that cloud rushed across . . . " (p. 87). In this example the first sentence of the paragraph belongs metonymically with the previous paragraph, which deals with the people present when Alex made his remark. Instead it encroaches upon the following paragraph, which is entirely discontinuous with the situation in which the remark occurs. What this montage, pivoting on "and," accomplishes is to juxtapose Alex's intuition of death onto Miss Fellowes's experience of it.

In *Party Going* other words besides "and" are pivots in the rapid montage taking place in the book:

[21] Robbe-Grillet, *The Voyeur,* p. 14.

And as she turned back Thomson went by with her luggage, light from his taxi curving over her head. She did not know, and he did not know she was there, he was taken up in his mind with how difficult it was going to be for him to find Miss Henderson and how most likely he would miss his tea. Meantime, as he was letting himself into his flat, Max was wondering if he would go after all.

[P. 19.]

The shifter "he" seems at first to refer to Thomson, since there has been repeated use of "he" and "him" referring to Thomson before this occurrence of the shifter. It creates a metaphorical equivalence between Max and Thomson, who are both in a quandary. This conceit, however, points up the significant difference between the two: Max can do what he wants; Thomson is bound to a responsibility.

Another example of the shifter is the use of "it" in the following passage: "There was that poor boy Cumberland, his uncle had been one of her dancing partners, what had he died of so young? One did not seem to expect it when one was cooped up in London and then to fall like that dead at her feet" (pp. 24–25). The "it" here conjoins young Cumberland's death and the fall of the bird. Further implications of this connection exist in the novel. There is a "Robin" Adams; Julia objects to Angela's calling Embassy Richard "Embassy Dick like any bird" (Embassy Richard is a relative of young Cumberland); in response to Edward's injunction to "pick up some bird, alive or dead," Thomson says, "Not wrapped up in brown paper . . . " (p. 159). The gratuitous death of the bird generates numerous echoes throughout the book.

The shifter "these" is also used:

Their porter then made difficulties and did not want to come with them; he would only offer to put her things in the cloakroom, so her young man, Robin, had to tip him in advance and so at last they too went in under into one of those tunnels. Descending underground, down fifty steps, these two nannies saw beneath them a quarter-opened door. . . .

[P. 9.]

"These" seems at first to refer to Robin, Miss Crevy, and the porter but really modifies "two nannies." Its ambiguous function is emphasized by the fact that it appears in a context that would normally suggest "the." The blandness of Miss Crevy and Robin seems to be equated with the mortuary quality of the two nannies.

The wittiest example of this deception occurs in the following passage:

> Also she felt encouraged and felt safe because they could not by any chance get up from below; she had seen those doors bolted, and through being above them by reason of Max having bought their room and by having money, she saw in what lay below her an example of her own way of living because they were underneath and kept there.
>
> "Aren't you glad you aren't down there?" she said, and he replied he wondered how it was going to be possible to get them out.
>
> "Have you ever been in a great crowd?" she said, because she had this feeling she must exchange and share with him.
>
> Down below Amabel broke into their silence by saying. . . .
>
> [P. 152.]

"Down there" plants the deception that is to occur with the phrase "down below": Max and Julia have been talking of the crowd outside the hotel ("down there"), whereas "down below" refers to the sitting room Max has hired. Because "down below" seems at first to duplicate the reference to "down there," we are deceived into visualizing the glamorous Amabel in the crowd outside.

The following sequence is an example of rapid montage without enjambment or a deceptive shifter word:

> "Have you ever been to Barshottie?"
>
> "No," she said, "why do you ask?"
>
> Miss Fellowes was better. She was having a perfectly serene dream that she was riding home, on an evening after hunting, on an antelope between rows of giant cabbages. Earth and sky were

inverted, her ceiling was an indeterminate ridge and furrow barely lit by crescent moons in the azure sky she rode on.

[Pp. 104–5.]

The effect of this passage is rather complex. The author's statement, "Miss Fellowes was better," seems to respond to Angela's question as to why Alex wants to know whether she has been to Barshottie. Both the fact that Miss Fellowes is better and the imagery of her recuperative dream seem to have a metaphorical relationship to Barshottie, Scotland. They are both indeed versions of the pastoral. The Barshottie landscape occurs as the last of three pictures on the walls of the hotel rooms. These three pictures are what Ricardou, after Gide, calls *"une mise en abyme,"* which is a play within a play or the inclusion in heraldry of one blazon within another.[22] The first picture, that of Nero fiddling, with eight fat women near him, is a caricature of Max and his women. The second picture, that of a girl being menaced by one man while another disappears behind curtains, is a caricature of Amabel being left to Embassy Richard while Max goes off. The third picture is that of a serene landscape in Barshottie—one of a few landscapes (including the inverted one of Miss Fellowes's dream) which occur as metaphorical possibilities in this fog-bound book. The stunning movement from inside to outside is a compositional motif in *Party Going.* The quiescent landscape of Miss Fellowes's dream (which needs no psychoanalytic elaboration) occurs after fits of delirium which seem to portend a stroke. Like other evocations of landscape in the book, it is part of a pastoral counterplot that evokes certain possibilities in the story's situation.[23]

[22] Ricardou, *Problèmes du nouveau roman,* p. 173.

[23] Although the fog outside the station and outside London is worse than it is inside the station and inside London, metaphorical evocations of landscape in *Party Going* reinforce our sense of claustrophobia within the fogbound station and the fogbound city. The seats in the bar are "like chrysanthemums with chromium plated stalks" (p. 23). When the station director looks out over the station, it "might" (Green does not

The use of enjambment also serves as a preparation for Robert's non sequitur and the coincidence that ensues. Robert has been sent to find Max; when he comes across Max in the bar, he denies that he has been sent to find him and says instead that he is looking for Miss Fellowes. No sooner does he realize that this remark is completely unmotivated (he *is* looking for Max) than he sees Miss Fellowes in the bar. As the book goes on, Robert often tries to make people realize how extraordinary this sequence of non sequitur and coincidence is, but no one is very impressed. His wife says to him: "Why are you always like this? Yesterday I asked you to put more coal on the fire and you passed me the egg" (p. 51). Robert keeps wondering whether there is "anything in" his having blurted out Miss Fellowes's name like that.

Perhaps the chapter is more nearly comparable to the poetic line (or verse) than is the paragraph, because it is a formal, graphic convention of the novel rather than a convention of formal discourse. The question is whether the chapter works

---

say that it does) look "like November sun striking through mist rising off water (p. 86). A summer landscape is also evoked (p. 149), as is a childhood landscape of bamboos (p. 47). Within the mortuary environment of the train station, this pastoral counterplot operates in the manner Empson discusses in *Some Versions of Pastoral.* Onto the grid of the pastoral, onto the grid of childhood, are imposed the complexities of adult relationships. Julia's charms, for example, are talismans against danger, perhaps against the kind of "sexual fit" Evelyn attributes to Miss Fellowes (p. 124). These charms—a pistol she once buried in a grove of artichokes, a top, and an egg with elephants inside which she thinks prevented her from being carried out to sea by an unfurled umbrella—are always associated with Julia's childish egotism. Whenever she wishes to talk about herself, she talks about her charms. Robert, on the other hand, discovers Miss Fellowes (who suggests progressive possibilities) within a similar landscape. Finally, the counterplot can evoke a ludicrous dissolving view of the characters: Amabel's "mountain face" (p. 176) is as ludicrous a metaphor as some of the figures in Ford Madox Ford's *The Good Soldier.* Her "hummingbird eyes" also verge on the ludicrous (p. 154); her comparison to an Okapi goes over the line (p. 140). At one point Max is described as an old buck being kicked to death by his women (p. 180), which evokes a marvelously ludicrous picture.

against the diachronic push of the story in the same way that the line works against the horizontal push of the sentence. Ricardou claims that typographical blanks can, without indicating any temporal hiatus in the fiction (the story), create a regular periodicity in which the temporary abatement of the story (effected by the termination of each chapter) foregrounds the act of writing which is habitually masked by the anecdote; and the continuity of the writing is itself contested by the regular architecture which the chapters provide.[24] One way to interpret Ricardou's statement that the fiction may be only a mediation of the conflict between "writing" and "architecture" is by Jean Cohen's notion of metaphorical "replacement." Cohen's thesis is that all the deviations he points to in his discussion of poetic language must be resolved metaphorically. There is consequently a kind of metaphorical replacement of the syntactic "displacement" committed by various poetic devices.[25] As the most conspicuous of the conflicts between the anecdote and the producing of the anecdote, the chapter can invite metaphorical or synchronic resolutions of diachronic displacements. Under the notion of displacement, I also include the phenomenon of the availability of motifs which are not earned by the logic of the story (for example, the repetition of the bird motif in *Party Going*).

The relation of one chapter to another varies along the vertical-horizontal, synchronic-diachronic axes. *Moll Flanders*, which is notably through-composed and invites no regression of attention, has no chapters at all. The only kind of regression which Dickens's novels invite is a function of inadequate memory—that is, we look back to another chapter to recollect what happened or to reidentify some character. In Dickens the chapter is a function of serial publication. In Henry Green's novels, by contrast, we are invited to oscillate backward and forward between chapters in order to note compositional changes and similarities. This invitation is made

[24] Ricardou, *Problèmes du nouveau roman*, pp. 161–70.
[25] Cohen, *Structure du langage poétique*, pp. 199–225.

chiefly by the compositional motifs we have been discussing, but in a novel like *Nothing* it is also made by configurations of characters and events.

Except for the mystery or adventure tale, where the pause at the end of a chapter is used for suspense, for teasing the reader's interest in the story, the chapter disrupts our involvement in the story, "unmasks" the anecdote. The first effect of the chapter is to provide an efficient "breathing" unit for the writer. As Green points out, referring to the Victorian novel:

> The reason for great tracts of prose in narrative was that the cinema, which has taught the modern novelist to split his text up into small scenes, had not in the days when Proust was writing and before yet exerted its influence. Accordingly, the novelist in those days, who had twenty, thirty pages or more to cover in a chapter, needed bridges to carry him from one moment of action to another, and the only reasonable bridge was a spate of moralizing or philosophy.[26]

Green's notion of "cutting" in the novel has its ancestry in Wordsworth's notion of "spots of time," Poe's discussion of the attention span, and Joyce's notion of epiphany. It becomes in Green's case (if not in Wordsworth's) part of an anti-expository bias. The second effect of the chapter, as we have pointed out, is to provide synchronic interest in the design of the book rather than involvement in its anecdote. Perhaps the most demanding use of the chapter is made in Henry James's *The Awkward Age,* which is one of the most difficult novels in the English language.

In *The Awkward Age* the novel approaches the condition of a play, but because this novel has a greater amount and complexity of material than a play would allow, it is obscure. Since, moreover, the world dealt with its unfamiliar, the difficulty of understanding what is going on is increased. What James does, however, to alleviate somewhat the demands of

[26] Green, "The English Novel of the Future," p. 22.

this objectivity, is to supply ten chapters, each of which is named after one of the characters. The chapters then provide nodes around which our baffled attention can gather, signals as to the way in which a given stretch of material is organized. For example, the first chapter, "Lady Julia," is named after a woman who never appears in the book and who is in fact dead. She is a specter haunting all that comes afterwards, an incontrovertible standard of judgment. Despite James's account of the *donnée* of this book (see his preface to *The Awkward Age*), we note that the real intrusion into the world of this novel is not that of Nanda (the young woman who is coming downstairs for the first time to join her mother's worldly circle) but that of Mr. Longdon (whose old-fashioned standards challenge the standards of this world).

The architecture of Robbe-Grillet's *The Voyeur* is quite different. The typographical blanks between its three sections are signals for something unknown having taken place. These hiatuses undermine the integrity of the story, call into question our assumptions about the sequence of events we have witnessed, as do the literal repetitions of events characterizing the opening pages of the novel. The architecture of this book, in other words, undermines the security that narrative continuity gives us and compels us to recompose a number of possible stories as we go along. The conflict between narrative and architecture makes the fiction (or story) a drama of narrative decision, which ultimately devolves upon the reader. Robbe-Grillet proclaims: "For, far from neglecting him, the author today proclaims his absolute need of the reader's cooperation, an active, conscious, *creative* assistance. What he asks of him is no longer to receive ready-made a world completed, full, closed upon itself, but on the contrary to participate in a creation, to invent in his turn the work—and the world—and thus to learn to invent his own life."[27]

In Henry Green's novels synchronic relationships between

[27] Alain Robbe-Grillet, *For a New Novel*, p. 156. The italics are Robbe-Grillet's.

chapters are achieved by the rhyming of compositional motifs and by common dispositions of more conspicuous elements of the novel. *Concluding* is divided into three distinct parts, between which a blank page indicates a lapse of time. Each part is divided into chapters, between which a typographical blank does not necessarily indicate a lapse or a progression in time. Chapters I and II of *Concluding* overlap (they take place at approximately the same time): Mr. Rock senses that above the fog, at some clear height, there is a flight of birds; in the second chapter Miss Edge sees a cloud of starlings rise from "her" woods and then hears the girls arising upstairs "with a sound of bees." In the first chapter, Mr. Rock predicts that it will be a fine day in the end; in the second chapter Miss Edge says grudgingly that the sun will shine (grudgingly because she and Miss Baker have to go to town). In the first chapter Mr. Rock and Mr. Adams discuss the possession of their cottages; in the second chapter Miss Edge and Miss Baker discuss their desire to have Mr. Rock's cottage. In the first chapter Mr. Rock and Mr. Adams "sluice through" woods that are covered with fog; in the second chapter Miss Edge views the woods and the fog through which Mr. Rock and Mr. Adams are coming. In Chapter I Mr. Rock and Mr. Adams hear the echo of someone calling "Mar-ee"; they discuss the problems of locating the echo's source, and Mr. Adams is mysteriously "relieved to hear just a girl hollering." In Chapter II Miss Edge thinks that she hears someone call, and when Miss Baker says that she does not hear anything, Miss Edge says mysteriously, "I wonder." These internal resonances create a reticulation of latent meanings and possibilities as the book goes on and pose subtle interior distances between us and the story. A mystery or adventure tale, on the other hand, does not permit any distance from the story, our closeness to which is increased rather than decreased by the use of chapters.

A much cruder interior distance between the reader and the story is created in Green's last two novels, *Nothing* and *Dot-*

ing, the choreography of which allows us no more involvement in the characters and their predicament than do the "turns" of a ballet. In an article on Green's late novels, A. Kingsley Weatherhead states: "The scenes of *Nothing* arrange themselves into patterns after the manner in which rhyming lines form patterns in various stanza formations or couplets. For the purpose of illustrating this phenomenon, I have considered as matching any two scenes in which there is an identity or a maximum of similarity between lengths, characters involved, and the topics of dialogue."[28] Following are his results: the first six scenes match as *a a b c c a;* the next four scenes are paired off into matching couplets. Weatherhead explains the incongruous third scene (*b*) as follows: "Of the scenes between the second and the sixth, the third is incongruous and matches nothing: this is devoted to a dialogue between Philip and Mary, two whose deeds and words lack the selection and polish that society requires, who contribute nothing to society and hence nothing to the pattern and symmetry dear to it."[29] In Part II, where the disposition of relationships is being disrupted and reorganized, there is no formal order among the scenes. In Part III order is again established, and Weatherhead's adumbration of the scenic alignments in this part resembles his adumbration of the first part. Employing John Crowe Ransom's distinction between "structure" and "texture," Weatherhead concludes:

Symmetry, and hence structure, is finally satisfied, but within it, the texture has exercised its rights. For the structure of *Nothing*, while it inevitably attenuates the liberty and autonomy of texture and tends to inhibit individuality and foster the stereotype, offers an essentially benevolent government. And texture can find its freedom, albeit a chartered one, in and according to structure. It does not have to run away and live it up in the woods.[30]

[28] A. Kingsley Weatherhead, "Structure and Texture in Henry Green's Latest Novels," pp. 116–17.
[29] Ibid., p. 118.
[30] Ibid., pp. 119–20.

Although Weatherhead's description of the "rhyming" among chapters is very helpful, his evaluation of *Nothing* (and *Doting*) is inadequate. In these books Green's ambition is to produce the kind of novel Henry James produced in *The Awkward Age*—a novel approaching the conditions of a play. But Green does not wish to write a play, to have actors and producers mediate between his work and the audience.[31] The effect of Green's architecture in these books is not to provide nodes for our attention but to mock the wills and actions of his characters. His is not the subtle irony directed against Mrs. Brook in *The Awkward Age;* his is farcical, because Green is not able or willing to evoke the complex issues surrounding the notion of civilization, of manners, which James is able to evoke so cogently. One notes, incidentally, that Green violates his prescription for a novel of pure dialogue rather obtrusively in these two novels. In *Doting* there are continual stage directions (especially regarding voice), which, because of their frequency and their lack of strategic importance, are more obtrusive than James's subtle stage directions in *The Awkward Age*. There are also in *Doting* two elaborate descriptions of a nightclub scene, at the beginning and at the end of the book, which, coupled with a seemingly gratuitous Saint Peter theme, are apparently supposed to give the book some realization not provided by the dialogue. In *Nothing* we have one very elaborate description, which is puzzlingly involute, and a few briefer descriptions. Edward Stokes gives an admirable summary of the stylistic disharmony in these books:

> Stylistically, *Nothing* reminds me of a pawpaw tree—a leafless, spindly-limbed plant out of which sprout, incredibly, and with no apparent relationship to the slender branches which can barely support them, and from which it is inconceivable that they can draw their sustenance, a few monstrous, globular fruit. That is what strikes one in reading *Nothing*—the disproportion, the lack of connection and relationship, the effect of lush, artfully designed

[31] Green, "The English Novel of the Future," p. 22.

patches of purple (or rather of white, rose and blue) arbitrarily superimposed on the abstract, colourless background. And as the colours, which in earlier novels had strong emotional resonance, have here become mere pictorial clichés, so the long sentences, which in earlier novels had flowered naturally and had almost invariably been of special thematic significance, have here become mere exercises in elaboration.[32]

In other words, texture does not really "exercise its rights" in these books as Weatherhead claims.

In discussing "creative description," a mode of description which generates affective associations as it goes along without being controlled by a particular idea or emotion, Ricardou says of the eroticism created by one novel: "One must underline an essential phenomenon here. Produced entirely by a writing which obeys formal directives, the eroticism in this case increases in density bit by bit. If it crosses this threshold and becomes a hypothetical meaning, it will cease being a *consequence* of description and will become its source of inspiration."[33] A similar threshold characterizes the use of chapters; if the repetitions between chapters become so obtrusive as to trivialize the act of narration, the novel becomes self-consciously minor. In Samuel Beckett's case a contestation of the story by the narrative is just barely maintained (the "barely" is constantly insisted upon by Beckett's narrators); the narrative seems to be always absorbing the story, which keeps reappearing. It is as if Beckett, having reduced *King Lear* to the storm and heath scenes, rehearsed many of the salient responses of Western civilization to the funny and terrible images of those scenes. In Green's last two novels, the narrative in turn seems almost absorbed by the architecture, by the choreography of scenes. After Green's earlier novels (and especially after *Loving*) it appears as if Green opted at

[32] Edward Stokes, *The Novels of Henry Green*, pp. 221–22.

[33] Ricardou, *Problèmes du nouveau roman*, p. 108. The italics are Ricardou's.

this time for *A Comedy of Errors* rather than for *As You Like It* or *Twelfth Night.*

Viewing the chapter as a formal, graphic unit in the novel comparable to the line or the stanza in poetry, let us note that there are no transchapter enjambments in Green's novels.

Since our final discursive figure involves tense, some of our material overlaps that in the previous chapter. Our interest in tense, however, concerns the shifting relationship between the axis of the narrative and the axis of the story. The narrative can make available to us, at any time in our reading, events which form an irreversible progression in the time of the story. The book by Green having the clearest diachronic commitments is his first, *Blindness,* the tripartite format of which signals a clear developmental curve: "Caterpillar," "Chrysalis," and "Butterfly." *Caught,* however, does not have such clear diachronic commitments. The dissonance between narrative time and fictional time (the time of the story) is indicated by the following phrase: "some months earlier, as will appear" (p. 10). This prolepsis, involving paradoxically an anticipation of the past rather than of the future, reminds one of Edwin Arlington Robinson's Merlin, who remembers forward. Like the shifters in *Party Going,* these disjunctions foreground the act of writing and defamiliarize our sense of the present instance.

Putting aside for a moment the agrammatical use of tense, the question of defining tense in the arts is rather complex. In the novel, for example, the narrative past tense is a fictive present tense in the sense that the narrated events occur as we read. They are not past events for the reader—they take place each time he reads about them. The narrative past tense is past, however, insofar as the reader is aware of work having been done on those events. That is, whenever the reader is aware of an expansion or a contraction of the narrative in relation to the fiction, he is aware of the "pastness" of the narrative past tense. Moreover, the awareness that one can reread is an integral part of one's reading experience. The film, on the other hand, has no real present tense—its action takes place in a kind of *temps imparfait* that makes any direct address to the audience jolting. The film, moreover, incorporates in its mimesis the technical means of repetition and continuation. In the theater, on the other hand, one can have absolute presentness, which has made violations of the proscenium clichés in contemporary theater.

The shift from past tense in *The Voyeur* to present tense in *Jealousy* indicates Robbe-Grillet's desire to eliminate the illusion of a denotative level of reality preceding the making of the book. In *Jealousy* we are attending the novel's making, according to certain internally consistent laws of association; we are not reading about events in a real world that the narrative is condensing or elaborating. The narrative *becomes* the fiction: "Thus the duration of the modern work is in no way a summary, a condensed version, of a more extended and more 'real' duration which would be that of the anecdote, of the narrated story. There is, on the contrary, an absolute identity between the two durations."[34] Green's polemic against mimetic responsibility (or against verisimilitude) is less radical. There is no tendency in Green toward the kind of situation we have in Beckett's *The Unnamable,* where the novel becomes a voice talking about the necessity to keep on talking. The disjunction between narrative and fiction in Green still assumes an a priori reality which is not pulverized by the reification of language or subject to the aleatory demon. Mr. Entwhistle's dread of cats in *Blindness* reminds one of the description of the banana trees in *Jealousy:* "I do hate cats, they frighten me so. There is something so dreadful about a cat, the way she seems to be looking at nothing. They don't see flesh and blood, they see an abstract of everything" (p. 130). Mr. Entwhistle would think Robbe-Grillet something of a cat.

Besides the prolepsis in *Caught,* Green uses other agrammatical shifts in tense in order to vary internal distances. The

[34] Robbe-Grillet, *For a New Novel,* pp. 152–53.

shift into the present tense moves one closer to the subject of the narrative—like the close-up in films:

> The cock was angry and he watched his hens for a moment with a sense of humiliation, one claw stopped in mid-air. . . . Everything was too soft—the sun, and the dew, and the gentle weeds. He wanted heat, heat. Between intervals of killing things on himself he stretched out his neck and told this to the world, and that he was king of this castle.
>
> Joan upstairs is putting on her stockings. What a lot of holes there are in them, but no matter. Sunday today. How will Father take the church bells? Last Sunday he had not minded very much. It is going to be beautifully hot, and Father will hate that too, poor old thing. George hated the heat, only she loved it. The wonderful sun!
>
> [*Blindness*, pp. 113–14.]

The following is another example of how shifts in tense affect the relation between foreground and background:

> She moves to a looking-glass and wrestles with her hair. In the glass was the brown-papered wall behind, the paper hanging in strips, showing the yellow plaster beneath. Those holes in the roof. And there was the rash that broke out in the top right-hand corner of the glass where the paint had come off the back. She was so miserable. The only chair has no back, and the front leg is rickety, so that you have to lean over to the right when you sit down.
>
> [Ibid., p. 115.]

A special instance of this movement is a shift into the present tense prelusive to direct discourse, which is absolute presentness:

> She was wearing rough tweeds, and she was smelling of soap, because it was near tea time.
>
> He turns his head on the pillow, the nurse rises, and Mrs. Haye walks firmly up the room.
>
> "Well, how are you?"
>
> [Ibid., p. 44.]

This shift in tense is agrammatical in the sense that it violates our normal grammatical expectation that a shift in tense indicates a shift in time. Green does not continue to use this device in later novels—perhaps because it is too closely parodied by the kinds of errors in shifting tense that are made in grammar school compositions.

Although the notion of agrammaticalness has precision only within the limits of a sentence, it helps to clarify deviations in fiction. Both those critics who applaud the notion of formal realism and those who decry it take the position that the so-called realistic or bourgeois novel has been and still is the norm for prose fiction. When a novelist, therefore, "lays bare" his devices,[35] when he draws our attention to the disparities between the axis of the story and the axis of the narrative, when he makes available to us motifs which are not earned by the chronological sequence of the story, when his prose clearly departs from the norm of reportage, he is deviating from the general norm of formal realism. To some extent, of course, all writers of any worth have made such departures, but modern writers make no attempt to disguise them. If the semiological fiction of Jean Ricardou represents a terminus, the surfaces of Henry Green represent an interesting way station.

[35] Victor Shklovsky, "Sterne's *Tristram Shandy*," p. 30.

V
Surfaces and Depths

The bottom of the sea is cruel.
[Hart Crane, "Voyages I," in *The Complete Poems and Selected Letters of Hart Crane* (Garden City, N.Y.: Doubleday Anchor Books, 1966), p. 35.]

There is an interesting conflict between the views of Victor Shklovsky and Georg Lukacs about the conspicuousness of artistic means in the novel. Shklovsky says of *Tristram Shandy:* "Sterne even lays bare the technique of combining separate story lines to make up the novel. In general, he accentuates the very structure of the novel. By violating the form, he forces us to attend to it, and, for him, this awareness of the form through its violation constitutes the content of the novel."[1] Lukacs, on the other hand, pointing to a gap between great epic and minor epic, says: "The subject's form-giving, structuring, delimiting act, his sovereign dominance over the created object, is the lyricism of those epic forms which are without totality."[2] Having commented upon the self-effacing subjectivity of great epic, in which the whole life of a society is revealed, and having censured the "self-created ruins" of Sterne, Lukacs discusses the function of verse in epic forms. Homer's verse is liberating because "a pre-stabilised harmony decrees that epic verse should sing of the blessedly existent totality of life; the pre-poetic process of embracing all life in a mythology had liberated existence from all trivial heaviness." In an age where immanent meaning has become a problem, only prose, with its "unfettered plasticity," can encompass the dynamics

[1] Victor Shklovsky, "Sterne's *Tristram Shandy,*" pp. 30–31.
[2] Georg Lukacs, *The Theory of the Novel,* p. 51.

of struggle and success: "In the world of distances, all epic verse turns into lyric poetry . . . for, in verse, everything hidden becomes manifest, and the swift flight of verse makes the distance over which prose travels with its deliberate pace as it gradually approaches meaning appear naked, mocked, trampled, or merely a forgotten dream."[3] This assessment of verse inverts Shklovsky's advocacy of laying bare one's devices; its plea for unselfconscious deliberateness underlies David Lodge's statement: "The circumstantial particularity of the novel is thus a kind of anti-convention. It attempts to disguise the fact that a novel is discontinuous with real life."[4]

From Lukacs's point of view some of Green's literary traits are lyrical short-circuitings of the novelist's quest for meaning. Green's books lack the elaborate and sustained metonymic achievements of Balzac and Tolstoy, whose works become metaphors for entire civilizations. His books lack what Lukacs calls "philosophy," which is a symptom of and an attempt to bridge the gap between inner and outer, self and world, the empirical and the intelligible. At least his ambitions in this respect are limited, intermediate. If the question generated by the epic is "how can life become essential?"[5]—to which Homer gave an answer before the question was formed—the questions generated by Green's books are less final and less detailed in their process of formulation. Green's gerundive and adjectival titles are disclaimers against the ambition for closure. The lack of exposition Green points to as characteristic of the novel of the future is accompanied, moreover, in Green's best novels, by poetic devices which evoke traditional humanistic problems without documenting their context. One might,

[3] Ibid., pp. 58–59. One is reminded by this discussion of the bridge that Sin and Death build to connect Hell and Earth after Satan realizes his fallen condition and before he experiences it to the full. There is implicit in *The Theory of the Novel* a notion of a "fall" from the world of the epic to that of the novel, a fall that, as in Milton, entails the possibility of maturation.

[4] David Lodge, *Language of Fiction,* p. 42.

[5] Lukacs, *The Theory of the Novel,* p. 35.

as we have said, extrapolate from Lukacs a wariness of Green's metaphoric short-circuiting of the cautious elaborations of prose and claim that the meanings arrived at by this method are unearned and idiosyncratic.

This quality of short-circuiting, of unearned meaning, seems to me to be more characteristic of allusive than of internal metaphors. By the former I mean metaphors which compare an item (*A*) within the work to another (*B*) outside it. By the latter I mean metaphors generated by the repetition or "rhyming" of certain motifs within the work, by which those motifs accumulate certain tones and meanings. In the latter case these metaphors will be effective only if the contexts in which the motifs appear are well realized. Otherwise, one may not be aware of the motif; or its repetition will seem abstract, algebraic, like the insertion of *x* in an equation. The same provisions are true regarding the validity of allusive metaphors, except that unearned allusive metaphors tend to be more seductive. The kind of metaphor I have in mind is one in which *B* has a rich cultural context which gives a false sense of meaning and profundity to *A*. An example is Edward Albee's *Zoo Story*, which, like *Who's Afraid of Virginia Woolf*, is not really about its putative theme. The play deals with a man named Jerry who, accosting another man named Peter on a park bench, proceeds to taunt and humiliate him until Jerry drives Peter to kill him. The major portion of this one-act play deals, however, with the horror of Jerry's life and specifically with sexual horror—in the form of a libidinous landlady and her dog ("malevolence with an erection"). Albee was not content, however, with writing a brief play about sexual horror but felt that he had to invest Jerry with social significance, a message-for-us-all. The facile way he does this is to make Jerry a parallel to Christ: Jerry impales himself on a knife, Peter cries "Oh my God," and Jerry says, "I came unto you . . . and you have comforted me." The stage direction "He laughs, so faintly," which occurs in place of the above ellipsis, anticipates the audience's ironic reaction to this pretentiousness. In other words, this motif is not realized in the play; it is only referred to.

Similarly, *Doting* contains a Saint Peter motif that provides a facile and overly crude irony, as if Green is not certain whether we have really appreciated the absurdity of his "doting" characters. It also seems to extend the significance of this doting to an entire civilization—an extension which the substance of the book cannot really bear. Arthur Middleton dotes on a young woman named Annabel Paynton; in retaliation Arthur's wife, Diana, almost has an affair with their friend Charles Addinsell; when things get too warm, Arthur passes Ann on to Charles, who is also unsuccessful in seducing her; in attempting to break up Charles's relationship with Ann, Diana introduces him to Ann's friend Claire Belain, whom he successfully seduces. Diana and Arthur have a son, Peter, who is something of a prig. At the end of the book, all the characters come together in a night club for a going-back-to-school party for Peter. The book ends, "The next day they all went on very much the same." The book is for the most part self-consciously flat, as we can see by examining the chapter endings (which, like poetic line ends, are salient places for rhyming). The second chapter of the book ends:

> He snored.
> "There, sleep my darling," she murmured.

The fifth chapter of the book ends:

> "There, sleep my darling," she mumbled.
> And in a moment or two he snored.

This formula, in its mindless connection of motifs (the reversal in sequence vitiates all but a temporal relationship), keeps our apprehension of the action on the surface. Similar chapter endings accomplish the same arresting of the attention at the surface. Chapter I ends with this sequence of dialogue:

> "So what?" Miss Paynton demanded.
> "Nothing" the boy replied.
> "Steak's cold" Mr. Middleton grumbled.
> "Darling, Peter was so hungry" his wife explained.

Chapter III, in which nothing of much consequence happens, ends with this sentence-paragraph: "Soon after this he paid the bill and they left without arranging to meet again." Most of the other chapters end with a similar flat sentence (often consisting of compound sentence patterns or predicates)—either of action or of dialogue.

The first and last chapters of the book, however, contain two elaborate descriptions of the night club in which the Middletons hold a party for Peter. In addition to the stylistic disharmony of these scenes, Green introduces a Saint Peter theme vis-à-vis Peter. During the book Peter is a fisherman, and Diane refers several times to the number of fish he has caught (he ends up with twelve). The night club where they gather is called Rome, where they are to watch some wrestlers as part of the stage show. At one point "a near miracle occurred," and they are served their meals. Peter keeps returning to his "goblet" throughout the meal. He at first wets himself with ice water from the wine bottle but later avoids this baptismal act by being more careful. Peter keeps saying "Oh God" through the scene and says it for the last time when a conjuror comes on stage. This evocation of Roman decadence and of a priggish and ineffectual Simon Peter is rather a heavy joke which undermines the delicate farce of the book.

Green's internal metaphors (or the rhyming of compositional motifs) are not short-circuitings of an expository process. Despite the fact that there are few compositional motifs in *Doting* and *Nothing*, there is also little exposition. If, according to Lukacs, man and his environment have become problematic in the novel, Green's reticence reflects or anticipates the further atomization of society. George Eliot's characters cannot be known in the way Achilles or Odysseus are known, but they can be investigated. Green's characters are problematic in two senses: we are very often not certain whether or not their substance is exhausted by their appearance; and if there is some residue which is not expressed by appearance, we can only approach it obliquely, through uneasy intuitions. Let me illustrate these phenomena.

One of the motifs in *Party Going* is that of surfaces and depths. During Miss Fellowes's delirium she is threatened with drowning by increasingly tempestuous waters. Robin is described as "drowning in his depth" (p. 37) as he struggles with his feelings for Angela Crevy. After discussing the value of fellow feeling, Thomson is described as pitying himself and the girl Emily (who has given him a friendly and unexpected kiss) as they cling together "on dim whirling waters" (p. 162). Amabel is pictured in the bathroom after having taken a bath: Her image is clouded over by steam, and only gradually, as her body turns from pink to white, does more and more of herself begin to be reflected (p. 175). The images of surfaces and depths have to do with two related problems: As stated above, are the characters in this novel so shallow that their substance is exhausted by their appearance? Is the positivist mode of the traditional novel discredited by the epistemological changes we discussed at the end of Chapter II? Is it not probable that the "age of suspicion" Nathalie Sarraute talks about is not restricted to literary conventions? that we distrust Balzac's psychological motivation and feel that it is at best an abstraction from a "smear of probabilities" and at worst a subsuming of individual actions under arbitrary commonplaces of human behavior? That is, the control an author exercises over our point of view makes us credulous regarding his authoritative explanations of behavior. It is this control, invested with the confidence of a strong authorial voice (Fielding's geniality, George Eliot's intelligence) that has come under fire in the modern novel. Many critics of Kafka will minimize the expository passages of *The Trial* (the parable of the gatekeeper and K.'s "realizations" at the end) to note the automatization of the subjective that is the *real* subject of the book. Camus's *The Stranger,* similarly, represents a "degree zero" of motivation. If characters are not exhausted by their appearance, their depth can only be intimated. The light of analysis in the modern novel, like the effect of light in some physics experiments, distorts the phenomena it is attempting to illuminate. One is reminded of Jacques Lacan's approach in his psychoanalytical writings, where the language of analysis becomes as dense as the language of the unconscious. Exposition becomes poetry.

The depiction of Amabel's image being clouded over by steam and reappearing as her skin turns from pink to white suggests the exhaustiveness of appearance. This phenomenon is summarized by Evelyna: "If people vary at all then it can only be in the impressions they leave on others' minds, and if their turns of phrases are similar and if their rooms are done up by the same firm and, when they are women, if they go to the same shops, what is it makes them different, Evelyna asked herself and then gave the answer: money" (p. 145). Regarding Amabel's inner life, one notes that she is capable of going to sleep immediately whenever she wants. Max is also exhausted by his appearance, an appearance which is not, moreover, completely reliable. All that we really know about Max is that he is rich, handsome, and idle, drinks a lot and sleeps with many women, and is not terribly careful about the way he spends his money. Part of Max's attraction, moreover, is "in his having started so well with someone even richer than himself" (p. 89). As it happens, however, he and the older woman with whom he is linked have never met.

After Julia tells Max about her charms and demands that he tell her about his childhood toys, Max considers it an "unlucky business" and makes up a toy doll to meet her expectations. His inner life is as follows: "When he thought, he was only conscious of uneasy feelings and he only knew that he had been what he did not even call thinking when his feelings hurt him" (p. 107). These feelings, moreover, seem to pertain almost exclusively to sex.

Julia is exhausted by her charms: expressions of her childish egotism and talismans against brutal reality. Like Max she is not one for words, i.e., for thought: "If she had no memory for words she could always tell what she had worn each time she met him. Turning over her clothes as they had been packed she was turning over days" (p. 45). Angela Crevy, the least "respectable" member of the group, is almost always referred to as "Miss Crevy" by Green. She is described as follows: "She was very pretty and dressed well, her hands were ridiculously white and her face had an expression so bland, so magnificently untouched and calm she might never had been more than amused and as though nothing had ever been more than tiresome" (pp. 26–27). In the following and last sentence of the paragraph, her "young man" is described: "His expression was of intolerance." Robin's exhaustibility is subtly indicated later in the book: "Meanwhile Mr. Robin Adams, Miss Angela Crevy's young man . . ." (p. 95). The redundancy of the full name, including the "Mr." and of his identification vis-à-vis Angela seems to underline the exhaustiveness of this identification. The images used to describe Angela and Robin (lilies in a pond, etc.) are subverted by "if you will" and "if you like," as if such metaphors were redundant or gratuitous.

Green underlines the shallowness of these characters by authorial comments on the identical furnishings of Max's and Amabel's apartments: "There were in London at this time more than one hundred rooms identical with these. . . . If people then who see much of each other come to do their rooms up the same, all one can say is they are like household servants in a prince's service, all in his livery" (p. 133). But Green combines this contextual (mimetic) phenomenon with the problem of narrative strategy by means of free, indirect speech. About Alex's reaction to Amabel's arrival, Green says: "In this way he showed how he had been taken in by Amabel, whose wish it was that she should not show haste. In this way also he showed again how impossible it is to tell what others are thinking or what, in ordinary life, brings people to do what they are doing" (p. 149). It is then problematic how much of the superficiality (in a nonpejorative sense) of Green's books is accounted for by the apparent superficiality of some of his characters or by his reticence toward probing human personality.

One of the essays in Robbe-Grillet's *For a New Novel* is entitled "New Novel, New Man," since Robbe-Grillet's account of the new novel is also an account of a cultural debacle—man no longer believing in a nature invested with values. Unable to assume the a priori consensus of the traditional novel, the modern novel creates its own significations as it proceeds. Robbe-Grillet's novels are novels of surfaces generated by an insistent regard. Although the novels consist of elaborate enumerations of objective details, and although Robbe-Grillet repudiates our traditional humanistic designs on the world and insists that objects must be presented in their otherness, the consciousness that views these objects is "the least neutral, the least impartial of men: *always* engaged, on the contrary, in an emotional adventure of the most obsessive kind, to the point of often distorting his vision and of producing imaginings close to delirium."[6] This kind of intelligence, like Benjy's in the first section of *The Sound and the Fury,* makes apparently for total presentness and surface. Such an intelligence is completely without self-reflexiveness and is fully defined by its impressions. To put the problem another way, the flatness of Robbe-Grillet's books is not too far from the flatness that would result from having *Bleak House* narrated by Mr. Krook. The social and psychic dislocations characterizing *Bleak House,* and the attendant obsessive behavior, are intensified in Kafka and in the nouveau roman.

Lucien Goldmann accounts for the gradual dehumanization

[6] Alain Robbe-Grillet, *For a New Novel,* p. 138. Italics are Robbe-Grillet's.

of the modern novel by pointing to the increasing reification of modern society. Though the liberal capitalist economy provided some area for individual initiative at the same time it took on a life of its own, further phases—involving the development of monopolies and especially the intervention of the state in the economy—have completed the individual's alienation from his environment, his sense that things have a life of their own.[7] Although England, bolstered by its empirical-pragmatic traditions, has tended to maintain traditional humanistic values more stubbornly in philosophy and literature than have Continental countries, a modern novelist like Green, as Nathalie Sarraute claims, cannot accept the bad faith of traditional novelistic exposition. Nor can he abide the "innocence" of Valéry's famous normative sentence, "La marquise sortit à cinq heures." In fact *Nothing* and *Doting* may partially be parodies of this norm: "The next day they all went on very much the same." Even in England modern novelists like Joyce, Woolf, and Green seem to sense the conflict between de jure humanistic values (of individualism, for example) and the reification which makes those values impossible to fulfill, which separates man from his environment. The penultimate chapter of *Ulysses* is written in a mode not unlike the mode of *Jealousy*—things taking on the agencing power abandoned by men. In *Finnegans Wake* man confronts the otherness of his language, just as man in the modern novel confronts the otherness of his environment. But Joyce has no real progeny except Beckett. If Henry Green rejects the legislative assurance of novelists like E. M. Forster, he maintains a measure of faith in the freedom of individuals. If his novels are realized by surfaces, those surfaces imply the problematic value of depths. Despite the internal laws we have discerned in Green's books, one seldom senses that their momentum comes from the act of describing, as Ricardou discusses it in his chapter on "creative description": "Thus a novel is for us less *the writing of an ad-*

[7] Lucien Goldmann, *Pour une sociologie du roman,* p. 111.

venture than the adventure of a writing."[8] It is noteworthy that there are numerous authorial intrusions in *Party Going* ("I" instead of "Eye"), which express a priori designs. At one point, for example, Green asks his readers' indulgence for his metaphorical descriptions, which are prefaced by "if you will" and "if you like" (p. 27). At another point he intrudes with an omniscient "as we shall see" (p. 134). The book in which he comes closest to Ricardou's creative description is *Back*, in which the name "Rose" generates an image of time-lapse photography of blooming and dying roses. It is notable that the hero and central consciousness of *Back* is suffering from war trauma, which he is obsessively reexperiencing.

We noted that Robin and Miss Fellowes drown in their depths, whereas Thomson and Emily, clinging together, are *on* "dim whirling water." For Green that dimness is a priori, to be evoked but not to be probed.[9] His usual tactic is to realize surfaces which suggest, without quite revealing, that dimness. In his book on Green, John Russell states parenthetically that "reflections and reverberations are Green's favorite devices for robbing space of its limits."[10] Just as linear description is the literary equivalent to (and defamiliarization of) visual perception, so the expansion and repetition of surfaces (with their accompanying pulsations of awareness) are Green's equivalents to (and defamiliarization of) the discursive probing of depths. A comparison of two passages will clarify this statement. In Chapter XX of *Middlemarch*, George Eliot gives a marvelous exposition of Dorothy's situation in Rome with her new husband. Description and interpretation are subtly modulated into each other as this account proceeds:

[8] Jean Ricardou, *Problèmes du nouveau roman*, p. 111. Italics are Ricardou's.

[9] The finest evocation of this theme of surfaces and depths in English and American fiction is *Moby-Dick*. The epigraph to this chapter has its ancestry in Melville.

[10] John Russell, *Henry Green*, p. 132.

> To those who have looked at Rome with the quickening power of a knowledge which breathes a growing soul into all historic shapes, and traces out the suppressed transitions which unite all contrasts, Rome may still be the spiritual centre and interpreter of the world. But let them conceive one more historical contrast: the gigantic broken revelations of that Imperial and Papal city thrust abruptly on the notions of a girl who had been brought up in English and Swiss Puritanism, fed on meagre Protestant histories and on art chiefly of the hand-screen sort; a girl whose ardent nature turned all her small allowance of knowledge into principles, fusing her actions into their mould, and whose quick emotions gave the most abstract things the quality of a pleasure or a pain; a girl who had lately become a wife, and from the enthusiastic acceptance of untried duty found herself plunged in tumultuous preoccupation with her personal lot. . . .[11]

Eliot gradually moves into the crisis in Dorothy's marriage, scrupulously examining the coordinates of her feelings. To penetrate thus into one of his characters would seem indecent to Green, who creates surfaces that suggest but do not "give away."

In the following scene from *Loving*, the description suggests the qualities latent in the characters' situation, but these qualities are held in suspension, qualified as the book goes on, without ever yielding to discursive translation:[12]

> "No," she said muffled, "no," as O'Conor's life was opened, as Kate let the sun in and Edith bent to look.
>
> What they saw was a saddleroom which dated back to the time when there had been guests out hunting from Kinalty. It was a place from which light was almost excluded now by cobwebs across its two windows and into which, with the door ajar, the shafted sun lay in a lengthened arch of blazing sovereigns. Over a

[11] George Eliot, *Middlemarch*, p. 143.

[12] The exposition I have discussed in *Party Going*, which has a higher proportion of such exposition than any other novel by Green, is minimal in ambition.

corn bin on which he had packed last autumn's ferns lay Paddy snoring between these windows, a web strung from one lock of hair back onto the sill above and which rose and fell as he breathed. Caught in the reflection of spring sunlight this cobweb looked to be made of gold as did those others which by working long minutes spiders had drawn from spar to spar of the fern bedding on which his head rested. It might have been almost that O'Conor's dreams were held by hairs of gold binding his head beneath a vaulted roof on which the floor of cobbles reflected an old king's molten treasure from the bog. . . .
. . . Then they were arrested by movement in the sunset of that sidewall which reflected glare from the floor in its glass.

For most of one side of this room was taken up by a vast glass-fronted cupboard in which had once been kept the bits, the halters and bridles, and the martingales. At some time O'Conor had cut away wooden partitioning at the back to make a window into this next chamber, given over nowadays to his peacocks. This was where these birds sheltered in winter, nested in spring, and where they died of natural causes at the end. As though stuffed in a dusty case they showed themselves from time to time as one after another across the heavy days they came up to look at him. Now, through a veil of light reflected over this plate glass from beneath, Edith could dimly see, not hear, a number of peacocks driven into view by some disturbance on their side and hardly to be recognized in this sovereign light. For their eyes had changed to rubies, their plumage to orange as they bowed and scraped at each other against the equal danger. Then again they were gone with a beat of wings, and in their room stood Charley Raunce, the skin of his pale face altered by refraction to red morocco leather.

The girls stood transfixed as if by arrows between the Irishman dead motionless asleep and the other intent and quiet behind a division. Then, dropping everything, they turned, they also fled.

[Pp. 53–55.]

I have quoted so extensively both because this is the richest scene in the book and because it is so unseamed in texture—even the brief ellipses seem rather a violation of its spell. Like the phenomenon of subliminal advertising, which immediately loses its effectiveness once we are made aware of it, the effectiveness of Green's surfaces depends on his ability to make us refrain from interpretation while the book goes on. If once we found the source of the echo in *Concluding,* the spell of the book would be lost.

We have discussed the use of internal metaphors in Green's novels to give intuitions of depth. In his article "A Novelist to His Readers," Green describes the related method of achieving depth by means of surfaces: "Where and how he places his characters in fiction is for the writer the context of his story. . . . The superimposing of one scene on another, or the telescoping of two scenes into one, are methods which the novelist is bound to adopt in order to obtain substance and depth."[13] This too is a form of metaphor, one example of which in *Party Going* is the movement back and forth between the chauffeurs Thomson and Edwards "down below" in the crowd and Max and Julia in an upstairs room in the hotel. Thomson, consigned to mind Julia's luggage in the crowd of people waiting for the fog to lift, gets a friendly kiss ("it's fellow feeling, that's what I like about it") from a strange girl. In the hotel Julia, who is childishly self-absorbed, says, "Poor Thomson . . . d'you think he's all right, and what about his tea?" She immediately seeks some reassurance from Max regarding their trip. We then switch back to Thomson, who is defending the girl's action against Edward's priggish objections and is extolling the virtues of fellow feeling (pp. 160–62). Just as the good-natured generosity of that kiss contrasts with the sexual sparring that occurs among the party-goers, the fellow feeling Thomson talks about contrasts with their mutual exploitation. Green's statement about depth reminds one of the special 3–D glasses that were used years ago in the movies to resolve superimposed images into three dimensions.

A variation of this use of montage is the cross-purpose dialogue, employed in *Loving* by Miss Burch and Mrs. Welch, and by Miss Burch and Nanny Swift. In one scene, as Miss

[13] Henry Green, "A Novelist to His Readers," p. 425.

Burch tries to interest Mrs. Welch in the erotic goings on between Raunce and her girls, Mrs. Welch keeps talking about her "little terror," Albert, who has just killed a peacock. The phrase "there you are" is a frequent gambit in Green for avoiding discourse or for shifting the grounds of conversation. Discussing the "mad Irishman" Paddy's possible wrath over Albert's act, Mrs. Welch says:

> "As to that I've only to pluck it . . . and 'e won't never distinguish the bird from a chicken they're that ignorant the savages. Mrs. Tennant can't miss just the one out of above two hundred. But I won't deny it give me a start."
>
> "There you are," Miss Burch said, "but listen to this. I was upstairs in the Long Gallery this morning to get on with my work when I heard a screech, why I thought one of the girls had come by some terrible accident, or had their necks broke with one of the sashcords going which are a proper deathtrap along the Passage out of the Gallery. Well what d'you think? I'll give you three guesses."
>
> "You heard me 'oller out very likely," Mrs. Welch replied, watching the door yet that Albert had shut behind him.
>
> [Pp. 49–50.]

Miss Burch's concern for Raunce's social and sexual aggressiveness is juxtaposed on Mrs. Welch's tacit admiration for her nephew's aggressiveness and her desire to protect him. In another scene Miss Burch's desire to air her grievances about Raunce and about Mrs. Jack (who has been "caught" in bed with Captain Davenport) is frustrated by Nanny Swift's desire to think the best of the situation and especially of her "little girl," Mrs. Jack. The nostalgia of Mrs. Welch and Nanny Swift for past times results in a syncopation of thoughts and memories (pp. 127–36). In another scene Mrs. Tennant and Mrs. Jack talk at cross purposes—Mrs. Tennant airing her grievances about the servants and Mrs. Jack interpreting many of Mrs. Tennant's remarks as characterizing her own adultery (pp. 196–203).

Another variation of montage, already discussed, is the *mise en abyme*. As Ricardou points out, the main story is often contested by the *mise en abyme*—as the action in "The Fall of the House of Usher" is contested by the story which the narrator reads to Usher, or as Oedipus' endeavors are contested by the pronouncements of the oracle.[14] In *Loving* Nanny Swift tells the children a story about six little doves that are poor and hungry and a "wicked tempting bird" who comes to the father to ask for the hand of one of the doves. While Nanny Swift tells them this story with shut eyes (just as she later shuts her eyes to what Miss Burch is trying to tell her about Mrs. Jack), the children witness the "quarrelling, murdering, and making love again" of the doves on the dovecot. The aggressive little Albert, after sardonically describing these goings on, threatens the girls by saying that he is going to bite off the head of one of the doves. "In the pub down in the country. There was a man there bit the 'eads off of mice for a pint" (pp. 55–61). Nanny Burch's story is an implicit injunction for the children to remain innocent of "quarrelling, murdering, and making love again," even as they are witnessing these life processes and even as the girls are coming under the sway of the tough, proletarian Albert.

The form of *Loving*, a fairy tale with "once upon a day," a missing ring, and "they lived happily ever after," is itself a kind of adumbrated *mise en abyme* contrasting with the exigencies of living and loving that become more apparent as the book goes on. None of the princes or knights in fairy tales, however, have indigestion—a sign in Green's novels of a constitutional rejection of life—like Charlie Raunce, who suffers from dyspepsia, exacerbated by his need for Edith and his venturing out-of-doors. (Similarly, Dale, the frustrated suitor in *Living*, has severe indigestion; Charlie Summers in *Back* has a block in his stomach; Richard Abbot in *Nothing* has choking fits. Charlie's compositional "death" at the end of *Loving* is a fall into experience, like the compositional injury which Merode

[14] Ricardou, *Problèmes du nouveau roman*, pp. 171 ff.

suffers in the "fallen world of birds" in *Concluding*. His murmured cry, "Edie," made in the tone with which Mr. Eldon cried out "Ellen" on his deathbed, is an anguished response to the plentitude of life Edith offers him. At the end Raunce and Edith do not live "happily ever after" in a kingdom purged of its dragons; they leave their castle (which, as Green tells us, is to be bombed anyway) to go to England, where a war is going on.[15]

A similar conflict between anecdotal flatness (best exemplified in the fairy tale) and the pulsing exigencies of life takes place at the end of *Back:* "So she had asked him to marry her, and had been accepted. She had made only one condition, which was that they should have a trial trip. So it was the same night, under Mr. Mandrew's roof, that he went to her room, for the first time in what was to be a happy married life" (p. 246). This anecdotal, anticipative flatness is contested by the mature awareness of the last sentences: "And she knew what she had taken on. It was no more or less, really, than she had expected."

The most obvious *mise en abyme* is the story of Sophie Septimanie de Richelieu, which occurs in the middle of *Back* and both parallels and contests the experience of Charley Summers. An eighteenth-century memoir narrates that Septimanie fell in love with a young nobleman but was forced by her father to marry a dull count of better family. The young man was killed, but subsequently Septimanie met his half brother, who was also his double. After Septimanie created a scandal at court by her feelings for the young man, he was done away with, and Septimanie pined away and died. Edward Stokes comments, "This parallel, like the legendary overtones, has the effect of universalizing the novel's central situa-

[15] As we shall see in the last chapter, this pattern is similar to the pattern which Todorov sees as characteristic of the novel in general: an infraction of the interior reality of the novel by the exterior reality of the social context. See Tzvetan Todorov, "Les catégories du récit littéraire," p. 150.

tion, of making it seem, not something merely bizarre and unlikely, but an archetype of human experience."[16] In an article on *Back*, Stephen Shapiro qualifies this statement:

The odd thing about Stokes' comment is that he neglects to specify the *content* of this archetype. Surely Stokes is not claiming that all men and women fall in love with the doubles of dead lovers and then fail to distinguish between the living and the dead. Charley's situation is universal only on an unconscious level. The "dead" lover we all know is the repressed memory of our erotic connection to our parents. The pressure past events exert on consciousness results in a partial fusion of past and present in the person of the loved object. When Septimanie and Charley fuse the dead with the living they are symbolically enacting—in an "abnormal" way—the "normal," unconscious process of choosing to love someone who represents a compromise between present possibilities and infantile desires.[17]

Both critics fail to see that the *mise en abyme* contests, as well as parallels, the main story. (If the archetypal dimensions of Charley's story are as clear as Shapiro thinks, why do we need a *mise en abyme?*) Shapiro makes the same mistake as A. Kingsley Weatherhead frequently makes in his book on Green: In interpreting *Back* Shapiro is insufficiently attentive to its surface, and he tends to reify some of his own figures of speech. For example, he states: "Charley's return home is ultimately to signify his rebirth. And the connection of birth with war, anxiety, death, and sex is quite provocative."[18] Rebirth is only Shapiro's way of describing Charley's development in the novel, but Shapiro then reifies his own figure by including it in a complex of elements that really are in the novel (war, death, anxiety, and sex). By this gambit he can now call our attention to a suggestive Freudian constellation. Shapiro criticizes Stokes and Russell for not getting at the "real" meaning

[16] Edward Stokes, *The Novels of Henry Green*, p. 119.
[17] Stephen A. Shapiro, "Henry Green's *Back*," p. 94.
[18] Ibid., p. 89.

of the title (which Shapiro takes as meaning back to the womb), but himself conveniently ignores the surface reference of the title, which is back from the war. It is clear from Green's autobiography, *Pack My Bag*, and from John Russell's article on him, "There It Is," that the war was a devastating experience for Green. Russell states:

So anyone familiar with his work would expect that war and fire would leave their mark on him. He was then thirty-five; first with his hands and lungs, afterward with his imagination, he had to come to grips with the fact of the whole place burning. But five more novels followed *Caught* and the three stories, and one might have supposed that in his imagination the War had receded. Without knowing him or knowing of his nightmare dreams at night, one could hardly be expected to realize how massive and lasting the effect of the War has been on him.[19]

This fact will enable us to see how the *mise en abyme* functions in *Back*.

The contestation between the main story and the *mise en abyme* is similar to that between the courtly love ethic and the realities of war and human nature in Chaucer's *Troilus and Cressida.* Unlike the loss of love in the eighteenth-century memoir, Charley's loss of love, and his obsessive reenactment of that deprivation, is part of an overall sense of loss and dislocation he is suffering after returning from the war. Similarly, in *Caught* Richard Roe has lost his wife, and this loss is a synecdoche for the generalized sense of loss he feels, just as the "heraldic deer" he sees are emblematic of life "before the revolution." In *Pack My Bag* Green associates war and sex:

Another story preyed on us then, and, as I have said before, one remembers only the horrible of times like those. It was the tale of the Germans being so short of fats they boiled their own dead down with ours to make food. This lie which we took for truth

[19] John Russell, "There It Is," pp. 437–38.

gave me exactly those awed feelings I had when we talked of sex. Sex was a dread mystery. No story could be so dreadful, more full of agitated awe than sex. We felt there might almost be some connection between what the Germans were said to have done and this mysterious urgency we did not feel and which was worse than eating human fats; or so it seems now, looking back on what many call their happiest time.

[P. 47.]

In *Caught,* where roses have constant erotic associations, and where erotic longings are constantly evoked by the stress of war, the following passage telescopes the themes of war and sex: "The air caught at his wind passage as though briars and their red roses were being dragged up from his lungs" (pp. 178–79). In fact, war is equated with sex when Prudence compares Pye's longing for her to a pilot's longing for his target: "War," she thinks, "is sex" (p. 119). At another point Richard Roe reflects that it would have been better to paint the fire engines "pink, a boudoir shade, to match that half light which was to settle, night after night, around the larger conflagration" (p. 149).

The equation "war is sex" translates as follows: since neither Green nor the characters in his novels have a sense of the totality of war, these novels—in Lukacs's terms—have lyrical rather than epic ambitions. Green attempts to translate the stress of war into personal-lyrical terms. War is sex or war is the loss of a loved one. The characters' experience of war is relatively dissociated from its socio-historical dimensions, as it is not in Stendhal, Tolstoy, or Sartre. Under the stress of war these characters are set adrift from their familiar modes of existence and are made to come to terms with their human separateness. Problems of sex, love, death, authority, and fellowship are defamiliarized by the disjunctions war brings about. In *Caught* Richard Roe says of Pye (who has committed suicide), "But it was sex finished him off, and sex arising out of his authority" (p. 195).

If the *mise en abyme* in *Back* relates the "twin attachment" or "extraordinary passions" that Septimanie felt for a young man and his double, and if her passion is defeated by the intrigues of the court, the main story moves from Charley's obsessive conviction that Rose has not died, that she and others are plotting to make him think that she is dead, to Charley's realization that the two women in the book are separate: "He felt that this was the final confirmation that Rose was truly dead, that Nance was a real person" (p. 155). At the same time we learn that Charley has gone through a literally unspeakable experience during the war and in a prison camp. Green's strategy in this book is similar to the strategies that A. Kingsley Weatherhead notes in *Loving, Nothing,* and *Concluding,* where characters deal publicly with private desires or anxieties by translating them into figurative terms that are decorous and manageable. In *Nothing,* for example, Jane Weatherby uses her daughter Penelope as a metaphor for her own desires and fears. As soon as these are resolved, Penelope is packed off to boarding school.[20] A similar process is at work in *Back:* "'Oh Rose, Rose,' he [Charley] cried out in himself, not noticing he did this without having real regret, 'Oh, why did you?' He began to cry, in his self pity seeing himself again with his hands, like a monkey's, hung up on the barbed wire which had confined him within the camp" (p. 210). As Mrs. Grant cries out at her husband's deathbed, "Come back," Green comments, "And the culmination of all this was about to remind Summers of something in France which he knew, as he valued his reason, that he must always shut out" (p. 218). The only occasion on which Charley speaks directly of his experience in the prison camp, he says, "I had a mouse out there" (p. 234). This remark is connected metonymically with his observation with Nancy of a cat and its kittens, and we recall that in Green's novels mice always have erotic associa-

[20] A. Kingsley Weatherhead, *A Reading of Henry Green,* pp. 125–26.

tions. Mr. Mead, Charley's employer, sums up Charley's plight: "It's sex is the whole trouble. There you are. Sex" (p. 221). Green's point seems to be that under stress certain areas of our experience (and especially the erotic) become kinds of neuralgic indices of that stress. The time-lapse effect of blooming and withering roses in *Back,* Charley's obsession with Rose, evokes his way of reenacting and managing the trauma he has suffered in war and his generalized sense of loss. As narrative strategy, moreover, this process is Green's way of evoking the quality of Charley's experience without having to plumb it.[21] Whatever the suggestive value of Shapiro's Freudian interpretation of *Back* in dealing with certain details, he does a disservice to the surface of Green's book by not dealing with it in its own terms. The *mise en abyme* in *Back,* like the play within the play in *Hamlet,* is a model for what the book is like in broad outline but what it is very unlike in realization.

A. Kingsley Weatherhead's book on Green is another example of a kind of interpretation that sacrifices surfaces for depths. Weatherhead says of his purpose:

> This study considers each of Green's novels and discovers some kind of order in the theme of self-creation. Characters emerge from childhood or other static situations, descend with whatever pains into the dark for the discovery of self, and break through alienation into community; or they partly proceed thus; or, faced with the opportunity, they altogether decline to. Then the order so discovered sometimes reveals in turn the significance of structures in the novels; and it offers a rationale for incident, imagery, and characters that are manifestly not of the "story" and do not contribute primarily to atmosphere.[22]

[21] For an alternative strategy in a comparable situation, see Andreyev's "The Red Laugh." The difference between the two works is like the difference between Frost's "The Mountain" and Hart Crane's "Island Quarry": Frost's narrator circles around the mountain; Crane's penetrates it.

[22] Weatherhead, *A Reading of Henry Green,* p. 3.

Weatherhead attempts to see Green's novels as concrete realizations of some of the abstract problems that one finds in such thinkers as Kierkegaard, Sartre, and Freud. In this sense his endeavor is like those of Umberto Eco, who sees literature as an "epistemological metaphor," and Lucien Goldmann, who thinks that both literature and philosophy are intelligibly related to the world view of a given social class. As we have pointed out, however, the effort to delimit the informing structure of a writer's work, to trace its structural analogies with other cultural phenomena, and to place this structure in a more global structure, which explains it, is an enormous undertaking. Despite Weatherhead's frequent perceptiveness, his sense of structure in Green's novels is faulty and warps his interpretations.

In discussing *Party Going*, Weatherhead says: "The sexual encounter is no mere animal comfort for the party as it is for Thomson, Julia's chauffeur, who seems to regard it as an alternative to tea. It is, or may be, a significant part of the process of self-creation." He then talks of the improper, narcissistic sexuality offered by Amabel as opposed to the proper sexuality (involving a mutual giving and taking) offered by Julia.[23] In this discussion Weatherhead is inattentive to the way in which the book actually works; in plumbing depths, he is inattentive to surfaces. We have pointed to the context of Thomson's sexual encounter and his notion of fellow feeling. In contrast, Julia comments to Max about the crowd below: "After all . . . one must not hear too many cries for help in this world" (p. 100). In contrast to Thomson's casual acceptance of a good-natured kiss, we have Green's ironically pedantic "explanation" of the motives behind Julia and Angela having kissed their "young men":

> Now both Julia and Angela had kissed their young men when these had been cross, when Mr. Adams had made off down in the station and when Max had stopped chasing Julia to sit in his chair.

[23] Ibid., pp. 45–46.

People, in their relations with one another, are continually doing similar things but never for similar reasons.

[P. 114.]

Angela's kiss is a form of dismissal; Julia's kiss is meant to "keep Max sweet" for the trip. Julia is no less self-absorbed than Amabel; her approach to men is simply different—child-woman instead of femme fatale. The passage Weatherhead quotes to show the mutual giving and taking that characterizes Julia's sexuality is more expressive of childish regression than of mature sexuality: "And as she hoped this party would be, if she could get a hold of Max, it would be as though she could take him back into her life from where it had started and show it to him for them to share in a much more exciting thing of their own, artichokes, pigeons and all, she thought and laughed aloud" (p. 255). The run-on sentence preceding this passage is, "So like when you were small and they brought children over to play with you and you wanted to play on your own then someone, as they hardly ever did, came along and took them off so you could do what you wanted." The willfulness of that sentence governs her designs on Max (whom she is going to "get a hold of").

Similarly, Weatherhead says that in *Party Going* Green chooses the metaphor of traveling to describe growth. As a matter of fact, he says that "The journey to the south of France tends to lose its real nature in accommodating itself to its archetypal function."[24] The novel, however, is not about a journey; it is about waiting to make a journey. The only journey that takes place in the book is that of Miss Fellowes, who, after her illness, "looked as if she had been travelling" (p. 247). The journey to France is outside the framework of the book, and in terms of archetypes one might as well (or better) take it as a metaphor for death than for growth. Julia (who dreams of childhood) and the effete Alex are the two characters in the book (except for the delirious Miss Fellowes) who

[24] Ibid., p. 51.

are most conscious of death. Alex thinks of himself as dead, a ghost driving through the streets (p. 37); later he thinks about the different qualities of dying depending on one's social class (p. 195). When Max lies about his whereabouts and says that he had to see his lawyer, Julia thinks that perhaps he had wanted to make out his will (p. 59); she then sees the hall of the station as a doctor's huge waiting room, similar to what it would be like when "they were all dead and waiting at the gates" (p. 59). One bit of montage that the book provides is the alternating descriptions of the claustrophobic Alex and Julia climbing the stairs of the hotel and of people carrying the ill Miss Fellowes up the stairs. The point is that traveling is *not* used archetypally in the book, or at least its context confounds any clear archetypal significance. Unlike Kim's journey in Rudyard Kipling's book (where the journey does signify a process of growth and discovery) or the journey in *Outward Bound* (which univocally signifies death), the journey in *Party Going* is, first of all, present only in an anticipative sense; second, it is only one of a number of similar journeys that Max has sponsored; and third, it comprises a number of elements. The fall of the pigeon at the beginning of the book is as much a journey as the flight of sea gulls out to sea which Julia takes as a good omen.

Even Julia's omen is ambiguous. "And now she remembered those two birds which had flown under the arch she had been on when she had started, and now she forgot they were sea gulls and thought they had been doves and so was comforted" (p. 161). It is noteworthy that Julia remembers having seen only two birds, whereas she really saw three (p. 19). Moreover, doves connote messengers of peace; gulls, scavengers. It is one of a few such substitutions in *Party Going:* The bird that falls at the beginning of the book is a "pigeon," but Miss Fellowes later refers to it as a "swallow," which can refer, with qualifying words, to birds of other families resembling swallows. It can thus refer to a variety of domestic pigeon (see the *OED* for this 1668 usage). The word "dove" was formerly applied to all the species of pigeon native to or known in Britain but is now restricted to the turtledove and its congeners (see the *OED*). Other birds which become part of this generic complex are sea gulls and geese (through metonymy, not through taxonomy). At one point Evelyn wonders whether the bird in brown paper would have been less odd if it had been a goose or another bird (p. 212). The missing bird (as three sea gulls [doves] become two) can only be the bird that tumbles to death at the beginning of the book. At another point Edwards says to Thomson, "Go on if you like and pick up some bird, alive or dead, Thomson, get yourself your cup o'tea if you feel like it." Thomson replies, "Not wrapped in brown paper . . . " (p. 158). The missing bird is associated with death, which is associated with a lack of fellow feeling; and it is this tacit equation that vitiates Weatherhead's interpretation of Julia's role in the book.

Weatherhead, in his search for a repressive parent figure in Green's novels, distorts the role of Miss Fellowes:

> The main business of the novel is the "departure" of young people for maturity. In a word, it concerns the death of youth, the abstract, which formerly had been presided over by the nannies and Miss Fellowes. Miss Fellowes now sees fit to watch over the death of youth and to grant it a decent burial. Her care of the pigeon figures her last proper function as a guardian of youth. But if she had finally disposed of it her usefulness would be at an end. She would be cast off, like nannies elsewhere in Green when their maturing protégés pass beyond their control. Naturally she seeks to protract her usefulness; hence she clings to the bird, clinging thereby to life itself.[25]

But it is clearly not life "done up in brown paper" that Miss Fellowes retrieves when she begins to feel better; it is death. The pigeon is not "only a local figure in a novel of which the large figurative structure now needs consideration."[26] It is the

[25] Ibid., pp. 46–47.
[26] Ibid., p. 47.

single most powerful compositional motif in the book—the fall of the pigeon dominates the atmosphere of this book as the echo dominates the atmosphere of *Concluding*. Miss Fellowes, as her name indicates,[27] is a touchstone for fellow feeling in the book, and the death of the pigeon signifies the death that the lack of, or warping of, that quality entails. The sexual associations of the pigeon motif are also part of a complex that includes fellow feeling, sex, and death. Most of the party-goers at one time or another abuse Miss Fellowes; Alex asks whether anyone really cares whether she dies or not (pp. 190–91). We noted earlier that the enjambments in *Party Going* prepared us for non sequiturs and coincidences: For no apparent reason Robert blurts out her name while he is supposedly looking for Max; moreover, no sooner does he mention Miss Fellowes than he sees her at the bar. Like the Ancient Mariner, Robert compulsively tells the story of this non sequitur and coincidence to anyone who will listen, but without making much of an impression. Robert thinks that he has found "his ruined temple" (the goal of his childhood games) in Max, but he really finds it in Miss Fellowes. It is the possibility of fellow feeling, unlooked for in the moral economy of Robert's circle, that he finds so uncanny.

In his commitment to an a priori psycho-philosophical scheme, Weatherhead commits similar distortions in his interpretations of other novels. He ignores their obvious rhetorical

[27] We are alerted early in the book to the possibility of word play with the characters' names. We note the redundancy of "Alex Alexander" and the assonance and echoing *n*'s of "Evelyn Henderson." We then note that Robert, whose name means "bright fame," has his last name mispronounced twice in the book; that Alexander, whose name means "defender of men," has little interest in women; that Amabel, whose name means "love beautiful," is the femme fatale of the book; that "Angela Crevy" suggests a craving angel, which is either a devil or a prig (Angela leans more toward the latter); that Robin is like the pigeon in being discarded and reclaimed in the book; and that the name "Richard," which has glamorous associations (it means "rich and strong"), belongs to a character who resembles the effete and epicene Alex.

strategies, like the metonymic linkages I pointed to in *Party Going,* where, in a sense, the central character is the absent Embassy Richard, emblematic of the futility of this party-going class. Despite his frequent perceptiveness (especially toward Green's last novels), Weatherhead sometimes masks what it is like to read these novels by the demands of a priori ideas. These demands, in turn, are uncontrolled by the socio-historical parameters that Goldmann posits in his sociology of the novel.

VI
Toward Loving

Annihilating all that's made
To a green thought in a green shade.
[Andrew Marvell, "The Garden," ll. 47–48]

Studies of the novel have tended to reflect two kinds of problems: those relating to the novel's ethical drive and those relating to its intrasystemic relations. Major work remains to be done, however, on the notions of form and context in the novel. To what extent are they metaphorical? To what extent do they lead us into false analogies with painting and sculpture? The degree to which recent attention to the interstices of writing and to the ideology of representation will change the retrospective dynamics of literary history remains to be seen.[1] Our own concern with the poetic tendencies of Green's work, however, has led us to a consideration of *Loving*. About this novel Edward Stokes writes: "In the first place, while I do not think that Green's vision has relaxed in *Loving*, this novel is not, it seems to me, his most important or most impressive novel. It is a masterpiece, but it is a minor masterpiece; it may be the most completely harmonious of Green's books, but it lacks the depth of psychological insight, the emotional resonance of *Caught*, *Back*, and *Concluding*."[2]

Stokes's gentle derogation of this novel stems from Green's "comic" vision: "Although *Loving* is clearly a much more important novel than *Nothing* and *Doting*, the fact that Green's vision in *Loving*, as in the other two novels, is essentially

[1] See, for example, Roland Barthes, *S/Z;* and Jacques Derrida, *De la grammatologie.*

[2] Edward Stokes, *The Novels of Henry Green*, p. 94.

comic, suggests that, for Green at least, the conversational method is viable only for not necessarily trivial, but certainly for un-tragic material and experience."[3] It seems to me that this critical vocabulary lacks any real cutting edge: Novels tend traditionally to resist the "tragic" classification since they characteristically deal with the adventitious. That is, a genre specializing in a documentation of circumstances is not easily assimilated to a mode that relentlessly carves out the essential. John O'Hara's *Appointment in Samarra,* for example, is actually undercut by its "tragic" format, which inadvertently ridicules the circumstances of the protagonist's death. What we often refer to in the novel as "tragic" are the kinds of ultimate conflicts that Irving Howe examines in *Politics and the Novel,* conflicts which seem to magnify the importance of individual decision. Such conflicts are seen nowhere in Green's works, which have little if any socio-historical ambition. Even in the two novels reflecting most clearly the impact of war, *Caught* and *Back,* neither the author nor the characters express any awareness of the socio-historical dimensions of the war. None of the characters make decisions reflecting political or ideological pressure. Green's novels are "comic" in two senses: (1) none of his characters are more formidable than Green's readers; and (2) his novels tend toward a reintegration of the individual into society, rather than his isolation from it. The protagonist of *Caught,* Richard Roe, overcomes his sense of dissociation through the common effort of fire fighting. He arrives at an understanding of his own experiences during the war partly by means of his sympathetic understanding of Pye, who is ruined by the authority that war confers on him. The protagonist of *Back,* Charley Summers, achieves at least a partial return back from the war. The anecdotal anticipation of a happy marriage at the end of the book is not unlike the "over in England they were married and lived happily ever after" that ends *Loving.* The reservations we have about the situa-

[3] Ibid.

tion at the end of *Loving* are not unlike the reservations we have at the end of *Back.* Although it is certainly true that the tone of *Loving* is rather different from the tone of *Back* and *Caught,* the difference is not that the latter two are more serious or more profound than *Loving;* it is that the tone of *Loving* is much more complex than Stokes takes account of. It is comparable to the nuances of tone characterizing *Twelfth Night* and *As You Like It,* plays which, if they are less intense than *Macbeth* or *Othello,* are more various. It is noteworthy that one of the few conspicuous false steps that Green takes is in the direction of tragedy. The theme of Pye's incest in *Caught,* which is supposed to dramatize the loss of personal security the war brings about, actually detracts from that theme, provides a fingerhold for the kind of interpretation Susan Sontag talks about pejoratively.

The problem of valuation, especially as it relates to the notion of depth, is very difficult. One gambit that is often used is to equate depth with inclusiveness. In that sense Thomas Mann, for example, would be a greater writer than Kafka. If, like Nathalie Sarraute, however, we take intensity as a standard of imaginative excellence, then Kafka is a greater writer than Mann. If we combine the two notions so that we are responding both to breadth of vision and intensity of realization, then the problem of valuation becomes more difficult, if also more productive. We do not really know very much about the effects novels have on our internal economy. It may be that *The Magic Mountain,* by virtue of the discursiveness that seems to give it so much scope, is actually limited by that discursiveness in terms of its transfer value; whereas *The Trial,* by its insistence on its own internal laws, has enormous transfer value. What I mean is that to some extent Mann's discursiveness exhausts the heuristic value of the experiences he creates, i.e., they have been annotated, so to speak; whereas the more seamless quality of Kafka's books makes them more effective heuristic wedges, i.e., they seem to provoke inquiry everywhere without satisfying it. Kafka stimulates the allegorizing movement of the mind without yielding to it.

It may be the very harmoniousness of *Loving*, its seamless quality, that deceives Stokes into underestimating its emotional carry-over. More than any other book by Green, *Loving* seduces the reader into suspending both interpretation and judgment until the book is finished. Recalling Green's dictum that "we seldom learn directly; except in disaster, life is oblique in its impact upon people," John Russell notes, "*Blindness*, *Caught*, and *Back*, different from the -ing novels, start from situations in which life's impact has been direct."[4] In rereading *Loving* I was reminded of the statement a philosophy professor once made in class: "You read Hume one day, and one night months later you wake up screaming."

Stokes's classification of *Loving*, *Nothing*, and *Doting* as "conversational novels" is highly misleading, even if it is statistically sound, for Green's narrative strategy in the novels up to *Nothing* and *Doting* is more homogeneous than Stokes makes out. Despite the differences in style, Green's achievement is that of a "lyrical" method[5] which "imprints" some of the intuitions we derive from the dialogue. Green's resourcefulness reaches its height in *Loving*, which contains three virtuoso descriptive passages telescoping many of our intuitions about the life of the book. The most important of these passages is the extended description of Paddy's room (pp. 53–55) that we have quoted in the preceding chapter; the others are the description of Kate and Edith dancing in the empty ballroom (p. 65), and the description of Edith surrounded by birds at the end of the book. Besides these set descriptive pieces, other descriptive elements register some of the intuitions we derive from the story. Virginia Woolf wrote of Hardy and Meredith: "This would seem to prove that a profound poetic sense is a dangerous gift for a novelist, for in Hardy and Meredith poetry seems to mean something impersonal, generalized, hostile to the idiosyncrasy of character, so that the two

[4] John Russell, *Henry Green*, p. 10.
[5] Ralph Freedman, *The Lyrical Novel.*

suffer if brought into touch."[6] In *Loving* Green attains his finest balance between the idiosyncrasy of character and the prepersonal qualities of experience—the dissolving view in *Concluding* of the submarine life of the impulses, and the "quarrelling, murdering, and making love again" in *Loving*. The former is achieved primarily by dialogue and story (though not exclusively); the latter is achieved primarily by description and by the disposition of certain actions.

The overall parabola of *Loving* is as follows: At the beginning of the book Mr. Eldon, the butler, is dying, attended by Miss Burch, the head housekeeper. As he lies dying, Mr. Eldon keeps repeating the name "Ellen." Since there is no blackout in Ireland, there are no blinds or curtains on the windows; yet he is almost completely isolated: "From time to time the other servants separately or in chorus gave expression to proper sentiments and then went on with what they had been doing" (p. 3). The sentence "Came a man's laugh" seems to come from a great distance, the omission of the structure word "there" creating a sort of syntactic hiatus. It is Raunce's laugh that intrudes into this deathbed scene, as Raunce later intrudes into other static scenes. During the enchanted scene in Paddy's room, Raunce suddenly intrudes: "The girls stood transfixed as if by arrows between the Irishman dead motionless asleep and the other intent and quiet behind a division. Then dropping everything they turned, they also fled" (p. 55). He intrudes on Edith and Kate dancing together: " 'The little bitches I'll show 'em,' he said and suddenly opened" (p. 65). He intrudes into a fake Grecian temple, where Edith is playing blindman's buff with the two girls and "Raunce's Albert": ". . . Raunce entered upon a scene which this noise and perhaps also his presence had instantly turned to more stone" (p. 123). The effect of these intrusions is ambiguous: On the one hand his aggressiveness, his purposefulness contrasts with static, almost enchanted scenes. On

[6] Virginia Woolf, "Phases of Fiction," p. 137.

the other hand, in the last scene, his presence seems to have a petrifying effect, and to dissipate the beauty of the other two. This, among other ambiguities, pervades the book and gives it its peculiar tone.

After Eldon's death Raunce successfully seeks his position in the household, an attempt that is opposed by Miss Burch (who was apparently in love with Mr. Eldon). She says to Raunce at one point, ". . . you'll never get a Mr. out of me not ever, even if there's a war on" (p. 16). In this respect Raunce's situation reminds me of Pye's in *Caught,* whose undoing is brought about by a sudden assumption of authority during the war. Kate also refuses to call him "Mr. Raunce," and agrees to do so only after Raunce has won Edith. When Miss Burch asks Raunce, "Would you be in a draught?" she is referring to what she considers Raunce's unmerited assumption of authority and responsibility (p. 13). At another point Raunce says to "his" Albert, referring to Mrs. Welch's investigation of some missing waterglass, "It won't wash your acting the innocent my lad. The moment she come in that door between the scullery and where we was sitting over our tea I could tell you felt the draught" (pp. 61–62). The draught is treacherous for Raunce's swollen glands and dyspepsia, which are symptoms of his assumption of authority as well as his loving.

Raunce is described as a "pale individual, paler now." In that respect he is like his pantry-boy Albert, who is always described as "looking sick" (p. 3). When Miss Burch is being most acidulous to Raunce she asks, "And how many months would it be since you went out?" (p. 15). Recalling Mr. Eldon's window at the beginning, we note that Raunce refers to the outside as the "wrong side of the window" (p. 24). At the end of the book he is on the "wrong side of the window," preparing to leave for England. Before the overwhelming vision of Edith surrounded by birds, " 'Edie,' he appealed soft, probably not daring to move or speak too sharp for fear he might disturb it all. Yet he used exactly that tone Mr. Eldon had employed at the last when calling his Ellen. 'Edie' he moaned."

Eldon, however, dies in the claustrophobic setting of his room, whereas Raunce leaves for England with Edith, where they live "happily ever after" (p. 248).

If what I have just described is the overall parabola of the story, its realization in terms of "insinuating" motifs is remarkably rich. In one respect the book deals with a dying feudal class, unable to maintain the social structure which gave it its viability. The one anticipative detail Green makes available to us is that the castle is eventually to be burned down (p. 65). This fact hangs over the book and lends a kind of funereal or nostalgic quality to the narrative. On the one hand the servants, in the midst of the dislocations caused by war, are trying to maintain some morale. During one of the scenes in which the servants discuss the question of duty and morale, Edith asks Raunce, " 'Well we're not crossin' over to the other side are we?' She looked sharp at him. He seemed dreamy." Raunce replies that they are not. " 'Not so long as we can find that ring. . . . And keep the house from bein' burned down over our heads. Or Mrs. Jack from running off with the Captain so Mrs. Tennant goes over for good to England' " (p. 176). On the other hand Mrs. Tennant, who is described as looking like a parrot at one point, blames generational differences on the servants. " 'I think everything's partly to do with the servants,' Mrs. Tennant announced as if drawing a logical conclusion" (p. 221). If Mrs. Tennant's name suggests a lack of real proprietorship, the castle itself is a kind of "eighteenth century folly in Eire" (p. 230), and the details of its decor are high tuba notes in the orchestration of the book. In the following description Raunce is a proletarian knight, traversing various landscapes to get back to his own "kingdom." Note that the "prize" that he brings back—"a withered trumpet"—like the social order he is trying to maintain, is dying:

In one of the malachite vases, filled with daffodils, which stood on tall pedestals of gold naked male children without wings, he had seen a withered trumpet. He cut off the head with a pair of nail clippers. He carried this head away in cupped hand from above thick pile carpet in black and white squares through onto linoleum which was bordered with a purple key pattern on white until, when he had shut that green door to open his kingdom, he punted the daffodil ahead like a rugger ball. It fell limp on the oiled parquet a yard beyond his pointed shoes.

[P. 10.]

The transformation of the withered trumpet into a rugger ball is a kind of synecdochic class survey. One notes also that in *Loving* the waning social power of this feudal class is accompanied by a waning sexual power. In view of the fact that the heir of the castle, Mr. Jack, is sexually effete, the withered trumpet may translate even further.

The play betwen the social and erotic themes of the book is enormously subtle. The refractions which motifs in *Loving* undergo remind one of Freud's notion of condensation, in which elements of a dream enjoy multiple representations in dream thought. If the equations we have discussed in Green's books (like "war is sex") have to do with the continuity between conscious and unconscious behavior and between public and private life, we can see that the lyrical mode is an acknowledgment of the integrity of man's being. If, as Charley Summer's boss in *Back* says, sex is the whole trouble, it is equally true that war is the whole trouble. One of the most brilliant scenes in *Loving*—when Raunce comes upon Kate and Edith dancing in an empty ballroom—indicates the condensation that the book achieves:

They were wheeling, wheeling in each other's arms heedless at the far end where they had drawn up one of the white blinds. Above from a rather low ceiling five great chandeliers swept one after the other almost to the waxed parquet floor, reflecting in their hundred thousand drops the single sparkle of distant day, again and again red velvet panelled walls, and two girls, minute in purple, dancing, multiplied to eternity in these trembling pears of glass.

[P. 65.]

The multiplication of images in the chandelier evokes the manner in which motifs in *Loving* are refracted into the related dimensions of the book's situation. For example, the peacocks are one element in the decor of the castle; in this respect they are almost museum pieces: "As though stuffed in a dusty case they showed themselves from time to time as one after another across the heavy days they came up to look at him" (p. 55). Their cries, however, provide a trombone accentuation of the erotic in the book. As Kate and Edith discuss what they would do if they found Raunce or "Raunce's Albert" in their room, the peacocks below begin to parade. When Edith gives a screech at one of Kate's suggestions, "A peacock screamed beneath but they were so used to this they paid no notice" (p. 40). A bit later, a "real outcry from the peacocks" signals the appearance of Mrs. Jack and Captain Davenport, who are having a passionate affair (p. 41). When Edith makes her first appearance in the book, she is wearing a peacock's feather in her hair and is carrying a "gauntlet" full of peacock's eggs, which she is going to use as an erotic charm (p. 5). Later in the book, at the beginning of his courtship of Edith, Charley bends down and picks up two peacock's feathers, which he offers to Edith:

> "Whatever should I do with those?" she asked low.
> "You wore one the week of the funeral," he replied.
> "Not now," she said. They walked on with a space between.
> [P. 94.]

The shriek of the peacocks is associated with other shrieks in the book. When Raunce enters the sickroom at the beginning of the book, violating the pathetic intimacy between Miss Burch and Mr. Eldon, Albert "looked to listen as for a shriek" (p. 4). Later on, Raunce is standing in front of a map of Ireland, the pointer of which is operated by a weathervane. Raunce notices that the arrow is stuck in one position, "with the arrow tip exactly on Clancarty, Clancarty which was indicated by two nude figures male and female recumbent in gold crowns. For the artist had been told the place was a home of the old kings" (p. 45). Mrs. Jack, walking in and noticing that the arrow is pointing to the place of her adulterous affair, breaks the pointer in her agitation to remove the guilty sign. Kate and Edith accompany Raunce to the works of the weathervane, where a live mouse is caught in the gear wheels. As Edith lets out a shriek and faints, the mouse responds in a "paper-thin scream" (p. 48). Mice are subsequently used as oblique references to the erotic, as when Mrs. Welch refers to Edith and Kate as "two legged mice" or Kate worries about a mouse in Paddy's room.

The peacocks are associated most closely with Paddy, the Irish lampman who takes care of them. Mistrusted as an Irishman (since in collusion with the I.R.A. he might murder everyone in the house), his thick Irish brogue is unintelligible to everyone except Kate, who is his sweetheart. One of the most amusing moments in the book occurs when Mrs. Tennant expresses disbelief that Raunce cannot understand Paddy. When Mrs. Jack admits that she cannot understand him either, Mrs. Tennant says: "But my dear it's not for us to understand O'Conor. . . . We don't have to live with the servants. Not yet" (p. 224). In view of her earliest sentiment that they are in "enemy country" in Ireland, this observation also reflects the relations between the Anglo-Irish and the Irish. Her statement about the servants comes after Paddy has locked up the peacocks and will not let them out. But, as Kate tells Edith, "Paddy's not what you suppose" (p. 211). In the virtuoso passage describing Paddy asleep in his room, he is depicted first as an ancient Irish king preserved in cobwebs. When Edith wants to make a crown for him out of the ferns in the corner, Kate asks, "You aim to make him a bishop?" But if Paddy is one of Ireland's legendary kings (and potentially a bishop, as Irish history unfolds), he is a somewhat decayed one. His "fine set of teeth" (p. 102) is rotten. Paddy is more, however. At the table, as the servants are discussing Mrs. Jack's sexual misadventure with Captain Davenport, ". . . a great braying laugh started out of the lampman. It swelled. It filled the room." The laughter is infectious: "These two girls did not giggle this time, they both deeply laughed" (p. 87). Paddy appears as a kind of satyr in this scene. Later, as Kate is combing his hair, "Paddy's enormous head began to show signs of order with parts of the tangle, which might have been laid by hail, starting to stand once more wildly on its own on his black beanfield of hair after a ground frost" (p. 97). Paddy appears here as a heathen god of the earth. In this respect Paddy's connection with the peacocks has to do with the life of the impulses that Green evokes so well.[7] But if his decayed teeth remind us of Raunce's constant injunction to "clean your teeth before ever you have anything to do with a woman," we can see that the effect of these motifs is ambiguous, as is Raunce's intrusion into Paddy's chamber, as is the ending of the book. When Edith asks Kate whether she is really considering taking Paddy as a husband, Kate replies, "There's nobody else. A girl gets lonely" (p. 211).

Let us note, finally, that when "Mrs. Welch's Albert," who is a proletarian tough, arrives at the castle, one of the first things he does is to strangle one of the peacocks. He subsequently comes to dominate the young ladies of the house. Later, when Kate is contemplating smearing herself with the

[7] Paddy has earlier been connected with the affair between Mrs. Jack and Captain Davenport. Paddy "knows Clancarty," as Kate points out. At Clancarty Captain Davenport "digs after the old kings in his bog." Edith knows that the last time Mrs. Jack had been over to view the excavations she had returned without her drawers. In view of this fact, the following exchange is strikingly like Harold Pinter at his funniest:

"That Captain Davenport? Now where would I have heard he seeks after treasure in a bog?"

He got no answer.

"Do they dig for it," he went on, "or pry long sticks into the ground or what?" he mused aloud.

"Are you thinking you'll have a go?" Kate said.

[P. 32]

peacock's eggs as an erotic charm, she says to Edith, "But if 'e came upon it Edie 'e'd strangle me." Edith responds smiling, "Like little Albert did to one of his peacocks?" (p. 213). These echoes and innuendoes provide the shimmering texture of the book.

Another motif that is subtly refracted in *Loving* is the theme of Mrs. Tennant's ring. Mrs. Tennant mislays a ring. Shortly afterwards she leaves the castle to go to England, leaving the servants in charge. An "I.R.A." man comes down to investigate the loss of the ring (he is from the "Irish Regina Assurance"), and as a result of his investigation he refuses to recommend that his company pay for the loss. The loss of the ring and Michael Mathewson's investigation throw the house into a turmoil from which it does not recover. One significance of the ring is expressed by Charley, when, in response to Edith's question as to whether or not they are going over to England, he answers, "No . . . we're not. Not so long as we can find that ring . . ." (p. 176). The ring, then, has something to do with Mrs. Tennant's authority and with the servants' sense of duty. After the loss of the ring, "Raunce's Albert," after a futile heroic gesture in taking the blame for its loss, goes off to join the air force, and Raunce and Edith eventually leave for England. Despite the fact that the ring is returned, its loss remains a source of great concern to Mrs. Tennant, who feels that she cannot trust the servants any more.

When the ring is lost Miss Burch states: "We shall have to make them open up the drains for us that's all . . ." (p. 68). This motif is then reiterated throughout the book. When Mrs. Tennant returns from England, Mrs. Welch (who has been using the household's fear of the Irish as a way of masking the quantity of gin she has been buying from the shopkeepers) tells Mrs. Tennant: "I happened to be stood by the larder windows when I 'ad a terrible stench of drains very sudden. Quite took my breath away. Just like those Irish I said to myself as I stood there, never to clean a thing out." The following exchange ensues:

"You don't imagine . . . ?" Mrs. Tennant began to ask. She sat down on a kitchen chair.

"A terrible stench of drains," Mrs. Welch repeated. "And me that thought we were goin' to have them all up while you was away with Mrs. Jack."

"The drains?" Mrs. Tennant echoed.

"That's what was said," Mrs. Welch insisted.

"Who said? I never gave orders."

[P. 191.]

The ring, the drains, and "I.R.A." motifs are juxtaposed in one of Green's marvelous passages of syncopated conversation. The household is in an uproar over the loss of the ring and the appearance of the "I.R.A." man, Michael Mathewson. Raunce claims that the insurance investigator is really an I.R.A. agent and that if he (Raunce) had answered the door instead of Bert, he would never have let him in. Miss Burch then "surprisingly" breaks out: " 'Then they'll needs must dig the drains up,' she cried in what seemed to be great agitation, 'I've said so all along now haven't I?' " While Raunce is reassuring her that there is no need for such extreme measures, Paddy (interpreted by Kate) states that Michael Mathewson could not have been an I.R.A. agent because they only use the back door (pp. 170–71). The I.R.A. agent (like the dog Badger) is a member of the underground. His "underground" activities are suggested by the shades of meaning the ring takes on, as well as by other motifs that interweave with the ring. When Michael Mathewson visits the castle he defines his job: "I come down when they claim a loss" (p. 157). One of the people who claims a loss in the book is Mrs. Welch, who has lost her waterglass, which Edith has taken. We note that Edith also finds Mrs. Tennant's ring, and that as much in the castle begins to fall apart Edith continues to blossom (not without some growing pains).[8] Mrs. Welch deteriorates as the book

[8] The ring, hidden under half an eggshell by "Mrs. Welch's Albert" (and thus connected with the peacock motif), is retrieved for Edith by "Miss Moira," Mrs. Jack's daughter, as a wedding present. When Edith

goes on. After she interrogates her girls about their relations with the tradesmen, she cries out, "Oh my waterglass" (p. 70). A little later, after she has complained to Miss Burch about the loss of the waterglass, the latter says that Mr. Eldon would have been able to recover it for her. Mrs. Welch replies, "Not what is short out of my jar he never could" (p. 70). One of the other situations that has thrown the household into confusion is the affair between Mrs. Jack and Captain Davenport. One recalls in connection with the underground that "Captain Davenport seeks after treasure in a bog" (p. 32); and that the peacock that "Mrs. Welch's Albert" strangles is first buried by Mrs. Welch, then recovered by the dog Badger, hung in Mrs. Welch's larder by Raunce, and finally stuffed in "Raunce's Albert's" boiler by Mrs. Welch.

The other underground investigator is the dog Badger. At the end of the book Raunce and Edith are discussing their impending departure. " 'Why look who's here,' she exclaimed. He opened his eyes and found Badger wagging his tail so hard that he was screwed right round into a crescent. The dog seemed deeply ashamed of something" (p. 247). The dog has appeared to them before, bringing Raunce the carcass of the peacock. If one of the nicest bits of metonymy in the book is the donkey that keeps following "Raunce's Albert" around (p. 151), a similar use of Badger reinforces the peculiarly ambiguous tone of the ending. Raunce (whose name suggests "rancid") has been described throughout the book as having the same unhealthy pallor as his pantry-boy Albert. His dyspepsia is a sign of his constitutional rejection of living and loving. In connection with the drainpipes motif, Raunce is described at one point as slipping "inside like an eel into its drainpipe" (p. 11). He is described as "gliding" (p. 64) and like "a ghost without a head" (p. 13). Like Nanny Swift, who

---

expresses confidence that Miss Moira will get her the ring, "Raunce halted when he heard this. He looked at her almost in alarm" (p. 190). The fact that "Miss Moira" should return the ring to Edith accords well with the fairy tale format.

on her deathbed is described in turn as gray and then blue about the lips (pp. 129–34), Raunce's face is described as "very white and green and grey" (p. 246), then as "an ugly purple" (p. 246). Charley says at one point, "I shouldn't wonder if you made fun of this as you've done before but I love you so much my stomach's all upset an' there you are" (p. 232). At the end, when a combination of the deterioration of the household, Albert's decision to join the air force, and Raunce's mother's implied disapproval of his remaining out of the war prompt Raunce's decision to go to England, Edith says to him, "You're fed up, Charley, on account of your stomach." Charley replies, "It's too bloody neutral this country is" (p. 237). Despite his inability to "digest" the life that is opening up to him, Raunce says, "Just lately I been wonderin' if my life weren't just starting" (p. 118). The ending expresses both the plenitude of life becoming available to him and the constitutional inadequacies he must overcome.

The peculiar tone of this book can be seen very clearly in one of its moments. Mrs. Welch participates in a number of its comic aspects. As I have said, she tries to frighten her "girls" out of having anything to do with the tradesmen because she is surreptitiously buying gin from them and charging it to the house. Her cross-purpose conversations with Miss Burch are very funny. But her deterioration is the most conspicuous sign of the deterioration of the house; her besotted denunciation of the household to Mrs. Tennant on the latter's return is the first direct challenge to Mrs. Tennant's authority and the first real betrayal among the servants. At one point, as she pours herself another measure of gin, she explains her behavior as follows: " 'For why?' she asked herself aloud, 'because it ain't no use' " (p. 112). In *Loving* one sees very clearly the phenomenon Todorov describes as a mutual infraction of the laws internal to the novel and the laws external to it.[9] Just as Raunce invades the scenes of almost enchanted beauty, the outside

[9] Tzvetan Todorov, "Les catégories du récit littéraire," p. 150.

world begins to invade the world of the castle more and more until Raunce is on the "wrong side of the window," and we know, for Green has told us, that the castle is soon to be bombed. The ambiguity of the ending has to do in part with this invasion of the outside world. On Mr. Eldon's deathbed there is a mass of daffodils, the properties of which are in dispute between Raunce and Miss Burch (Raunce connecting them with hay fever). The mass of daffodils gives a suffocating effect to the room, and Raunce's gesture of kicking the daffodil foreshadows his leaving the castle.[10] The ending of the book, however, allows another interpretation—one of failure rather than success. The shame attributed to Badger would then be an uncovering of the shame implicit in Raunce's abandonment of the castle when the effort to keep things together becomes too strenuous. Shortly before Raunce decides to leave the castle, he lectures Kate and Edith on their responsibility to their masters. At the end he chooses to leave without giving any notice.[11]

Even the "loving" of the book has a deceptive surface. In the previous chapter we discussed the *mise en abyme* in *Loving* —Nanny Swift's story by the dovecot, which contests the "quarrelling, murdering, and making love again" that the children are watching. We also noted the fairy tale format of the book as a kind of implied *mise en abyme*. Underneath much of the comedy of the book (which has to do with the idiosyncrasy

[10] Flowers are used in *Loving* with still another nuance. As Raunce is preparing to invade the ballroom where Kate and Edith are dancing, "He picked this [a bowl] up, set it aside, then dipped his fingers in the rustle of potpourri which lay within. Walking on again he sniffed once at his fingers he had dabbled in the dry bones of roses and to do this was a habit with him the last few times he was over in this part" (p. 64). This gesture, as we can see even more clearly in a passage from *Blindness*, has the effect of taking oxygen: "She passed through the Great Hall. She buried her head violently into a pot of dead roses" (p. 88).

[11] One of the most striking examples of this phenomenon of infraction is the ending of *Lord of the Flies*, where the appearance of the ship's officer changes the whole scale of values the book has created.

of character and the vapidity of social forms) there is a struggle that comes under the heading of "quarrelling, murdering, and making love again." As Nanny Swift's story begins, Raunce comes out of an unused door in the castle wall. Later in Nanny's story Edith and Kate come out. Like Raunce they signal the children to be quiet, using a gesture which the children imitate. When Kate and Edith ask the children where Raunce is, Nanny Swift comes to this part of the story: "And then they were in great peril every mortal one" (p. 58). This peril is insinuated throughout the story, having to do with a complicated sexual competition that we sense in the book. As Raunce is approaching the ballroom where Edith and Kate are dancing, " 'What are they up to now?' he asked half under his breath. 'What's Edith after?' he repeated. He was grave all of a sudden" (p. 64). He is described as "like the most silent cat after two white mice," and he says to himself, "The little bitches I'll show 'em . . ." (p. 65). When Charley leaves the ballroom this sequence ensues: " 'Well would you believe that?' Edith murmured half giggling. But Kate was looking at her like she might have been a stranger and she stopped. 'All right come on,' Kate said vicious, 'we're not goin' to stay here all night are we?' " (p. 67). When Edith says in the midst of this scene, "It's over now," there is the implication of something unstated, something taking on the aspect of a spell.[12] One notes also that the detail of Kate's "gimlet" eyes occurs twice in connection with Edith's relationship with Raunce. We have talked about the connection of spells and sexuality in relation to *Concluding*.

As in *Concluding*, the world of *Loving* is full of echoes (the refractions of the two girls in the ballroom scene are a visual equivalent to the "Mar-ee" echo in *Concluding*). In one respect the echoings and mimickings in the book foreground the idiosyncrasies of speech and manner that differentiate people most conspicuously. As Raunce begins to suffer under his feel-

[12] I was reminded of "Cristabel" by this scene—by Edith's apparent "start" out of a spell and by Kate's "gimlet" eyes.

ings for Edith, his "surface manner" appears less and less often. Toward the end of the book Raunce states: "The way things are shapin' it wouldn't come as a surprise if places such as this weren't doomed to a natural death so to say." Edith replies: "Go on with you. . . . Why if Mrs. Tennant loses all her dough there'll always be those that took it. Don't you tell me there isn't good pickings to be had in service long after our children have said thank you madam for the first bawlin' out over nothing at all that they'll receive." Green then says, "She was beginning to speak like him" (p. 237). In another respect echoings seem to allude to the preconscious wellsprings of personality. Sometimes, as in *Concluding*, there are echoings of one character by another which seem to stretch verisimilitude a bit, as when Edith quotes Raunce's line, "There's many a time I'd give her a long bong jour" (p. 216). These echoings evoke the kind of hesitation in the reader that Todorov talks about in connection with the genre of the fantastic.[13] That is, we can assume a hiatus in the narrative that would account for the echoings or we can interpret these echoings figuratively. As figures they allude in both *Concluding* and *Loving* to the life of the impulses underlying personality. If the source of the echo in *Concluding* lies in the direction of a "fallen world of birds" or a lake in which someone has drowned, the source of the reflections in *Loving* is the whirling figures of Kate and Edith, whose description reminds one of the primal energy revealed by Merode's knee in *Concluding*. In both descriptions it is as if an atom has been split. These allusions in turn remind one of the incident which I believe is seminal in Green's work: the Hunt Ball in which a young man is persecuted by some girls because he has complimented one of them. Green says of the incident, "It must be a question of the sun" (p. 227). That sun (or lack of it) is emblematic of the institutional repression which Green traces in the British public school, in an incomprehensible war, in a deadening

[13] Tzvetan Todorov, *The Fantastic*.

civil service, and in a vestigial class system. The "stink" or decay in *Loving* stems from the same lack of human solidarity associated with Miss Fellowes's illness in *Party Going.*

In terms of the shallower "depths of psychological insight" Stokes discerns in *Loving,* it seems to me that what he is responding to is the subtle interior distance separating us from the characters (this distance does not become farcical, as in *Doting* and *Nothing*). Stokes notes in a chart tabulating Green's use of certain techniques that in *Loving, Nothing,* and *Doting* there is no "informal character revelation"—that is, no attempt to record the thoughts and impressions of characters as they occur, whereas this method is used in the percentages of 17, 21, 15, 16, and 17 in his other books.[14] In *Loving,* as a consequence, we are at a distance from the characters' interior life, which is insinuated into our awareness by the reticulation of compositional motifs. The characters' "presence" (which I am using in the sense almost of stage presence) is imprinted in our awareness by their characteristic speech patterns and by what Keats calls "stationing." He says about Milton, "He is not content with simple description, he must station—thus here we not only see how the Birds *'with clang despised the ground,'* but we see them *'under a cloud in prospect.'* So we see Adam 'Fair indeed and tall—*under a plantane*'—and so we see Satan *'disfigured—on the Assyrian Mount.'* "[15] This kind of stationing in *Loving* brings Green's characters alive. The final description of Edith is a marvelous example of stationing, and it includes elements that have acquired enormous suggestive power throughout the book (note that previously the doves and the peacocks have been associated through the detail of their "ruby eyes," one of Green's vivid color registrations).

Accordingly she picked up the bag of scraps. She began to feed the peacocks. They came forward until they had her surrounded. Then

[14] Stokes, *The Novels of Henry Green,* p. 75.

[15] Written in Keats's copy of *Paradise Lost.* Quoted in Walter Jackson Bate, *The Stylistic Development of Keats,* pp. 48–49.

a company of doves flew down on the seat to be fed. They settled all over her. And their fluttering disturbed Raunce who reopened his eyes. What he saw then he watched so that it could be guessed that he was in pain with his great delight. For what with the peacocks bowing at her purple skirts, the white doves nodding on her shoulders round her brilliant cheeks and her great eyes that blinked tears of happiness, it made a picture.

[P. 248.]

The stationing is enhanced by the choreography of Green's prose. The paragraph having moved deliberately in short sentences from detail to detail, the sentence unit begins to expand and the tempo of the prose to increase with sentence six, with Raunce's awakening to this brilliant scene.

The boundary between poetry and prose has always been a shifting one, like the boundary between literature and all that is not literature. Aristotle warned poets against the scientific poems of Empedocles and the kind of epic closest in form to the traditional novel (the biographical or chronological epic). The latter was inartistic because it lacked a rigorous structuration of events; the former was unpoetic because its cosmic drama did not center around the actions of man. Poetry for Aristotle was concerned primarily with human praxis; it was more philosophical than history, not because it approached the universals of metaphysics, but because it constituted a typology of human responses to critical human situations. If "fiction" eventually covers what Aristotle meant by "poetry," the realistic novel reflects his enlightenment poetics. Although the traditional novel assumes the biographical or chronological form derogated by Aristotle, although its circumstantial particularity masks its conventions, the topoi of realistic fiction reflect the centrality of man and the significance of human action. Epic ambitions have been undermined, however, in modern fiction by the growing reification of Western society, by the sense (articulated most dramatically by Michel Foucault) that man has become the object of social structures rather than the subject of his own history. Joyce's psychic and linguistic automatisms are indicative of this decentralization of man, as is the voided Haggada of Kafka's works. Even as much of the novelist's traditional authority for a documentation of experience has passed to the social scientist, the place of man in the social sciences has been called into question. What the lyrical mode of modern fiction restores is Schiller's notion of play—creative activity least subject to the expropriations of one-dimensional society.[16] What *Loving* may offer to the retrospective dynamics of modern literature, to the poetic freedom demanded by the nouveau romanists, is the greenest of thoughts in the greenest of shades.

[16] One can now purchase wallpaper covered with graffiti.

APPENDIX

Plot Summaries of Green's Novels

Blindness (written while Green was still a schoolboy at Eton and published in 1926) is about a young man named John Haye who, while returning home from his public school, is blinded by a stone thrown by a small boy at the train window. The novel deals with John's efforts to reintegrate his life and with his maturation from the supercilious schoolboy we see in the first section of the book. John's stepmother, Mrs. Haye, is instrumental in his recovery, sacrificing their country home in order to move to London, where John feels he can become a writer. The novel has a subplot dealing with a girl named Joan Entwhistle and her father (an alcoholic ex-minister) who live as social pariahs in a dilapidated house.

Living (1929) deals with life in a Birmingham factory. Old Mr. Dupret, the owner of the factory, is now bedridden, and his callow son takes over its management. The basic conflict in the book is between young Mr. Dupret and Mr. Tarver, the engineer, on the one hand and the older workers on the other hand. Among the latter are Mr. Bridges (known as "'Tis 'im" by the men), the works manager; Tupe, Mr. Bridges's spy; Mr. Craigan, the oldest and best molder in the factory; and Mr. Gates, a braggart and poltroon who, with his daughter Lily, lives in Mr. Craigan's household. When old Mr. Dupret dies, the older workers are dismissed. Other characters in the book are Bert Jones, a young man with whom Lily unsuccessfully runs away; Jim Dale, Lily's ineffectual suitor, who lives in Mr. Craigan's household; Mr. and Mrs. Eames, a happy and procreative couple; and Hannah Glossop, a jejune society girl with whom young Dupret falls in love. Concomitant with the conflict in the factory is Mr. Craigan's loss of authority in his household.

Party Going (1939) deals with a group of wealthy Londoners who are fogbound in a train station while waiting to depart for the South of France. The sponsor of the party, Max Adey, is an enormously rich young man. Other members of the group are Julia Wray, a spoiled young woman with whom Max hopes to have an affair; Angela Crevy, an attractive young woman who is at the margin of social acceptability; her boy friend Robin Adams (who is not coming on the trip); Evelyn Henderson, who is the young "old maid" of the group; Claire and Robert Hignam, other members of Max's circle; Alex Alexander, who, as his name indicates, is redundantly epicene; Amabel, the glamorous femme fatale of the book, from whom Max is trying to escape; Miss Fellowes, Claire's aunt, who becomes sick at the beginning of the book; and Embassy Richard, whose petty imbroglios are endlessly discussed and who finally makes an appearance in the last pages. There are also Thomson and Edwards, Julia's and Max's chauffeurs respectively; and a mysterious man, with a variety of accents and mannerisms, who is "always interfering."

Caught (1943) deals with the experiences of Richard Roe, who is apparently from Green's own social class, in the Auxiliary Fire Service during the war. Richard is a widower, whose son Christopher lives in his father's country house with Richard's sister-in-law Dy, with whom Richard has an anticipative sexual relationship. The book is unusual for Green in that it leaps backward and forward in time: Christopher had been kidnapped by the sister of Richard's fire instructor (and eventual superior) Pye, who is later destroyed by the pressures of his new authority. Under these pressures he becomes dependent on a woman named Prudence, whose favors he expensively shares; and he suffers increasingly from the delusion that he once had incestuous relations with his sister, who is in a mental hospital. At the end of the book, Richard's new-found maturity is indicated by his sympathetic understanding of Pye and his sense of camaraderie with men from a lower social class. Other characters in the book are Hilly, a girl from the fire station, with whom Richard has an affair; Chopper and Shiner, regular firemen; old Piper, whose resourcefulness in looking out for himself results in an undermining of Pye's authority; and Mary Howells, who has a mentally ill daughter and is also resourceful in looking out for herself.

Loving (1945) deals with the relations among servants, and between servants and masters, in an Irish castle during the war. At the beginning of the book Eldon, the old butler, dies and Raunce, the footman, successfully claims his place. He meets resistance from Miss Burch, the head housekeeper, and from Mrs. Welch, the cook. Raunce falls in love with one of the maids, Edith, with whom he is eloping as the book ends. The other maid, Kate, is involved with Paddy, the Irish lampman, whose speech can be understood only by Kate. Other characters are Mrs. Tennant, the owner of the castle; Mrs. Jack, her daughter-in-law; Captain Davenport, with whom Mrs. Jack is having an affair while her husband is at war; Mrs. Welch's tough little proletarian nephew, Albert; Nanny Swift, who took care of Mrs. Jack as a child and now takes care of Mrs. Jack's little girls; Raunce's pantry-boy, Albert, a callow young man whose ineffectuality contrasts with the tough aggressiveness of Mrs. Welch's Albert; and Michael Mathewson, a lisping insurance investigator whom Raunce takes (or pretends to take) for an I.R.A. man.

Back (1946) is concerned with the efforts of Charley Summers, a veteran returned from the war with an amputated leg, to readjust to civilian life. Obsessively concerned with the loss of his loved one, Rose, he meets Rose's half sister, Nancy Whitmore, who resembles her. After suspecting through most of the book that the people around him

(Nancy, Rose's husband James, Rose's father Mr. Grant, Charley's landlady Mrs. Frazier, and a ubiquitous acquaintance named Arthur Middlewitch) are in collusion to disguise the fact that Rose is alive and is in fact Nancy, Charley comes to accept Rose's death and is engaged to Nancy Whitmore at the end. Other characters are Mrs. Grant, who is severely disorganized psychologically until Mr. Grant becomes sick; Dorothy Pitter, Charley's secretary, with whom James sleeps because Charley is too slow to sleep with her; and Ridley, Rose's son, who Charley mistakenly thinks may be his.

Concluding (1948) deals with an old scientist, Mr. Rock, who (sometime in the future) lives retired at a state school that trains girls to be civil servants. Miss Edge and Miss Baker, the elderly spinsters who run the school, want to remove Mr. Rock from his cottage (which the state has granted him for life). Other characters are Rock's neurotic granddaughter, Elizabeth; Elizabeth's lover, Sebastian Birt, who teaches at the school; Miss Marchbanks and Miss Winstanley, frustrated spinsters; Mr. Adams, the woodman; Mrs. Blain, the cook; and a bevy of girls whose names begin with "M" (Mary, Moira, Merode, Marion, etc.). Two of the girls, Mary and Merode, have disappeared; when Merode is found, she cannot account for her disappearance or for the whereabouts of Mary. This mystery is unresolved when the book ends.

Nothing (1950), the first of Green's two dialogue novels, is about the affairs of wealthy middle-aged Londoners after the war. John Pomfret, a middle-aged widower, is having a waning affair with Liz Jennings. Jane Weatherby, an old flame of John's, is having a similar affair with Richard Abbott. John's daughter Mary and Jane's son Philip, who are both civil servants, decide to get married. Philip especially is rather priggish and humorless. By cleverly procrastinating in making definite plans about the wedding, and by playing on the priggishness and velleities of her son, Jane breaks up the proposed marriage. Instead, she marries John Pomfret. Jane has a daughter, Penelope, whom she uses to express her own wishes and anxieties. Throughout the book an old friend, Arthur Morris, is gradually being eroded by surgery.

Doting (1952) has to do with the infatuation of a middle-aged man, Arthur Middleton, for a young woman named Ann Paynton. In retaliation Arthur's wife, Diana, almost has an affair with their friend Charles Addinsell. When things get too warm for Arthur, he introduces Ann to Charles in order to get her off his hands. Charles, like Arthur, tries unsuccessfully to seduce her. Diana, attempting to break up this relationship, introduces Charles to Ann's friend Claire Belaine, whom Charles successfully seduces. At the end they are all together at a party given for Arthur's priggish son, Peter, who is going back to school. The social class of these characters is the same as that of *Nothing* and *Party Going*, and they are the only books by Green which are limited primarily to this class.

WORKS CONSULTED

Allen, Walter. *The Modern Novel.* New York: E. P. Dutton and Co., 1965.

Aristotle. *Poetics.* Translated by Gerald F. Else. Ann Arbor: University of Michigan Press, 1967.

Auden, W. H. *Collected Shorter Poems, 1927–1957.* New York: Random House, 1967.

Auerbach, Erich. *Mimesis.* Translated by Willard Trask. Garden City, N.Y.: Doubleday Anchor Books, 1957.

Barthes, Roland. *Critical Essays.* Translated by Richard Howard. Evanston, Ill.: Northwestern University Press, 1972.

———. *Elements of Semiology.* Translated by Annette Lavers and Colin Smith. New York: Hill and Wang, 1967.

———. *Mythologies.* Selected and translated by Annette Lavers. New York: Hill and Wang, 1972.

———. *S/Z.* Paris: Editions du Seuil, 1970.

———. *Writing Degree Zero.* Translated by Annette Lavers and Colin Smith. New York: Hill and Wang, 1968.

Bate, Walter Jackson. *The Stylistic Development of Keats.* New York: Humanities Press, 1962.

Beerbohm, Max. "The Guerdon." In *Parodies,* edited by Dwight MacDonald, pp. 147–49. New York: Random House, 1960.

Benveniste, Émile. *Problèmes de linguistique générale.* Paris: Gallimard, 1966.

Bierce, Ambrose. *The Collected Works of Ambrose Bierce,* Vol. 2. New York: Neale Publishing Co., 1909.

Booth, Wayne. *The Rhetoric of Fiction.* Chicago: University of Chicago Press, 1967.

Burke, Kenneth. *The Philosophy of Literary Form.* New York: Vintage Books, 1957.

Caudwell, Christopher. *Illusion and Reality.* New York: New World Paperbacks, 1967.

Chomsky, Noam. *Syntactic Structures.* The Hague: Mouton and Co., 1957.

Churchill, Thomas. "*Loving:* A Comic Novel." *Critique* 4 (1961):29–38.

Cohen, Jean. *Structure du langage poétique.* Paris: Flammarion, 1966.

Coleridge, Samuel Taylor. *Selected Poetry and Prose.* Edited by Elisabeth Schneider. San Francisco: Rinehart Press, 1971.

Cosman, Max. "The Elusive Henry Green." *Commonweal* 72 (September 1960): 472–75.

Daiches, David. *The Novel and the Modern World.* Rev. ed. Chicago: University of Chicago Press, 1960.

Dante Alighieri. *The Divine Comedy.* Translated by Charles Eliot Norton. Cambridge, Mass.: Houghton Mifflin Co., 1941.

Defoe, Daniel. *Moll Flanders.* Edited by J. Paul Hunter. New York: Thomas Y. Crowell Co., 1970.

Derrida, Jacques. *De la grammatologie.* Paris: Les Editions de Minuit, 1967.

Eco, Umberto. *L'Oeuvre ouverte.* Translated from the Italian by C. Roux de Bezieux. Paris: Editions du Seuil, 1965.

Eliot, George. *Middlemarch.* Edited by Gordon S. Haight. Cambridge, Mass.: Riverside Press, 1956.

Else, Gerald F. *Aristotle's "Poetics": The Argument.* Cambridge, Mass.: Harvard University Press, 1967.

Empson, William. *Some Versions of Pastoral.* Norfolk, Conn.: New Directions, 1960.

Forster, E. M. *Aspects of the Novel.* New York: Harcourt, Brace & World, 1954.

Foucault, Michel. *The Order of Things.* [Anonymous translation.] New York: Vintage Books, 1973.

Freedman, Ralph. *The Lyrical Novel*. Princeton, N.J.: Princeton University Press, 1963.

Freud, Sigmund. *The Interpretation of Dreams*. Translated by James Strachey. New York: John Wiley and Sons, 1963.

Friedman, Norman. "Point of View in Fiction: The Development of a Critical Concept." In *The Novel: Modern Essays in Criticism*, edited by Robert Murray Davis, pp. 142–71. Englewood Cliffs, N.J.: Prentice-Hall, Inc., 1969.

Genette, Gérard. *Figures*. Paris: Editions du Seuil, 1966.

———. *Figures II*. Paris: Editions du Seuil, 1969.

Geulincx, Arnold. *Annota ad Metaphysica*. In J. P. N. Land, *Arnoldi Geulincx Antverpiensis Opera Philosophica*, vol. 2, pp. 296–307. The Hague: Martinus Nijhoff, 1891–93.

Girard, René. *Deceit, Desire, and the Novel*. Translated by Yvonne Freccero. Baltimore: Johns Hopkins Press, 1965.

Goldmann, Lucien. *Pour une sociologie du roman*. Paris: Gallimard, 1964.

Green, Henry. *Back*. New York: The Viking Press, 1950.

———. *Blindness*. New York: E. P. Dutton and Co., 1926.

———. *Caught*. New York: The Viking Press, 1950.

———. *Concluding*. New York: The Viking Press, 1951.

———. *Doting*. New York: The Viking Press, 1952.

———. "The English Novel of the Future." *Contact* 1 (August 1950): 21–26.

———. *Living*. London: The Hogarth Press, 1964.

———. *Loving*. New York: The Viking Press, 1949.

———. *Nothing*. New York: The Viking Press, 1950.

———. "A Novelist to His Readers." *Listener* 44 (9 November 1950): 505–6.

———. "A Novelist to His Readers." *Listener* 46 (15 March 1951): 425–27.

———. *Pack My Bag*. London: The Hogarth Press, 1952.

———. *Party Going*. New York: The Viking Press, 1951.

Hall, James. "The Fiction of Henry Green: Paradoxes of Pleasure-Pain." *The Kenyon Review* 19 (Winter 1957):76–88.

Hartman, Geoffrey. "Milton's Counterplot." In *Milton: A Collection of Critical Essays,* edited by Louis L. Martz, pp. 100–108. Englewood Cliffs, N.J.: Prentice-Hall, Inc., 1966.

Herbert, George. *The Poems of George Herbert.* New York and London: Oxford University Press, 1907.

Hoffding, D. Harold. *A History of Modern Philosophy.* Translated by B. E. Meyer. Vol. I. London: Macmillan and Co., 1908.

Howe, Irving. "Fiction Chronicle." *Partisan Review* 16 (October 1949):1047–55.

———. *Politics and the Novel.* Greenwich, Conn.: Fawcett, 1967.

Huxley, Aldous. *The Art of Seeing.* New York and London: Harper and Brothers, 1942.

Jakobson, Roman. "Linguistics and Poetics." In *Essays on the Language of Literature,* edited by Seymour Chatman and Samuel R. Levin, pp. 296–322. Boston: Houghton Mifflin Co., 1967.

Jakobson, Roman, and Halle, Morris. *Fundamentals of Language.* The Hague: Mouton and Co., 1956.

Jakobson, Roman, and Lévi-Strauss, Claude. " 'Les Chats' de Charles Baudelaire." *L'Homme* 2 (1962):5–21.

Kant, Emmanuel. *Critique of Judgment.* Translated by J. H. Bernard. New York and London: Haffner Publishing Company, 1968.

Karl, Frederick R. *A Reader's Guide to the Contemporary English Novel.* New York: The Noonday Press, 1967.

Kenner, Hugh. *Samuel Beckett: A Critical Study.* Berkeley and Los Angeles: University of California Press, 1968.

Labor, Earle. "Green's Web of Loving." *Critique* 4, no. 1 (1961):29–40.

Leavis, F. R. *The Great Tradition: George Eliot, Henry James, Joseph Conrad.* New York: New York University Press, 1967.

Lessing, Gotthold Ephraim. *Laocoon.* Translated by Ellen Frothingham. New York: The Noonday Press, 1969.

Levin, Samuel R. *Linguistic Structures in Poetry.* The Hague: Mouton and Co., 1964.

———. "Poetry and Grammaticalness." In *Essays on the Language of Literature,* edited by Seymour Chatman and Samuel Levin, pp. 224–30. Boston: Houghton Mifflin Co., 1967.

Lévi-Strauss, Claude. *Structural Anthropology.* Translated by Claire Jacobson and Brooke Grundfest Schoepf. New York: Doubleday Anchor Books, 1967.

Lodge, David. *Language of Fiction: Essays in Critical and Verbal Analysis of the English Novel.* New York: Columbia University Press, 1966.

Lubbock, Percy. *The Craft of Fiction.* New York: The Viking Press, 1957.

Lukacs, Georg. "Ein Brief an Leo Popper." In *Die Seele und die Formen,* pp. 1–39. Berlin: E. Fleischel & Co., 1911.

———. *The Theory of the Novel.* Translated by Anna Bostock. Cambridge, Mass.: The M.I.T. Press, 1971.

Marcuse, Herbert. *One-Dimensional Man.* Boston: Beacon Press, 1968.

Melchiori, Giorgio. *The Tightrope Walkers: Essays of Mannerism in Modern English Literature.* London: Routledge & Kegan Paul, 1956.

Norden, Eduard. *P. Vergilius Maro Aeneis Buch VI.* Leipzig and Berlin: B. G. Teubner, 1926.

Ohmann, Richard. "Literature as Sentences." In *Essays on the Language of Literature,* edited by Seymour Chatman and Samuel R. Levin, pp. 398–411. Boston: Houghton Mifflin Co., 1967.

Ortega y Gasset, Jose. *The Dehumanization of Art and Other Writings.* Garden City, N.Y.: Doubleday Anchor Books, n.d.

Phelps, Robert. "The Vision of Henry Green." *Hudson Review* 5 (Winter 1953):614–19.

Prescott, Orville. *In My Opinion.* New York: Charter Books, 1963.

Quinn, Kenneth. *Virgil's Aeneid: A Critical Description.* Ann Arbor: The University of Michigan Press, 1968.

Rahv, Philip. "Fiction and the Criticism of Fiction." *Kenyon Review* 18 (Spring 1956):276–99.

Ricardou, Jean. *Problèmes du nouveau roman.* Paris: Editions du Seuil, 1967.

Riffaterre, Michael. "Describing Poetic Structures: Two Approaches to Baudelaire's 'Les Chats.'" In *Structuralism,* edited by Jacques Ehrmann, pp. 188–220. Garden City, N.Y.: Doubleday Anchor Books, 1970.

———. "Interpretation and Descriptive Poetry," *New Literary History* 4 (Winter 1973):229–56.

———. "Le poème comme représentation," *Poétique* no. 4 (1970), pp. 401–18.

———. "The Self-Sufficient Text." *Diacritics* 3 (Fall 1973):39–45.

Robbe-Grillet, Alain. *For a New Novel: Essays on Fiction.* Translated by Richard Howard. New York: Grove Press, 1965.

———. *Jealousy.* Translated by Richard Howard. New York: Grove Press, 1965.

———. *The Voyeur.* Translated by Richard Howard. New York: Grove Press, 1958.

Robert, Marthe. *Kafka.* Paris: Gallimard, 1960.

Russell, John. *Henry Green: Nine Novels and an Unpacked Bag.* New Brunswick, N.J.: Rutgers University Press, 1960.

———. "There It Is." *Kenyon Review* 26 (Summer 1964):433–65.

Ryf, Robert. *Henry Green.* New York: Columbia University Press, 1967.

Ryle, Gilbert. *The Concept of Mind.* New York: Barnes and Noble, Inc., 1949.

Sarraute, Nathalie. *The Age of Suspicion: Essays on the Novel.* Translated by Maria Jolas. New York: George Braziller, Inc., 1963.

Scholes, Robert, and Kellogg, Robert. *The Nature of Narrative.* New York: Oxford University Press, 1968.

Schorer, Mark. "The Real and Unreal Worlds of Henry Green."

New York Herald Tribune Book Review, 31 December 1950, p. 5.

———. "Technique as Discovery." In *The Novel: Modern Essays in Criticism,* edited by Robert Murray Davis, pp. 141–60. Englewood Cliffs, N.J.: Prentice-Hall, Inc., 1969.

Shapiro, Stephen A. "Henry Green's *Back:* The Presence of the Past." *Critique* 7 (1964):87–96.

Shklovsky, Victor. "Art as Technique." In *Russian Formalist Criticism,* edited by Lee T. Lemon and Marion J. Reis, pp. 3–24. Lincoln: University of Nebraska Press, 1965.

———. "Sterne's *Tristram Shandy:* Stylistic Commentary." In *Russian Formalist Criticism,* edited by Lee T. Lemon and Marion J. Reis, pp. 25–57. Lincoln: University of Nebraska Press: 1965.

Sontag, Susan. *Against Interpretation.* New York: Dell Publishing Co., 1969.

Southern, Terry. "The Art of Fiction XXII, Henry Green." *Paris Review* 5 (Summer 1958):61–77.

Steiner, George. "Last Stop for Mrs. Brown." *The New Yorker,* 12 July 1969, pp. 83–91.

Stevens, Wallace. *The Collected Poems.* New York: Alfred A. Knopf, 1957.

———. *Opus Posthumous.* New York: Alfred A. Knopf, 1966.

Stokes, Edward. "Henry Green, Dispossessed Poet." *The Australian Quarterly* 28 (December 1956):84–91.

———. *The Novels of Henry Green.* New York: The Macmillan Co., 1959.

Taylor, Donald S. "Catalytic Rhetoric: Henry Green's Theory of the Modern Novel." *Criticism* 7 (1965):81–99.

Tindall, William York. *Forces in Modern British Fiction, 1885–1956.* New York: Vintage Books, 1956.

Todorov, Tzvetan. "Les catégories du récit littéraire." *Communications* 8 (1966):125–51.

———. *The Fantastic: A Structural Approach to a Literary Genre.* Translated by Richard Howard. Cleveland: The Press of Case Western Reserve University, 1973.

Tomashevsky, Boris. "Thematics." In *Russian Formalist Criticism,* edited by Lee T. Lemon and Marion J. Reis, pp. 61–95. Lincoln: University of Nebraska Press, 1965.

Toynbee, Philip. "The Novels of Henry Green." *Partisan Review* 16 (May 1949):487–97.

Untersteiner, Mario. *The Sophists.* Translated by Kathleen Freeman. New York: Philosophical Library, 1954.

Valéry, Paul. *The Art of Poetry.* Translated by Denise Folliot. New York: Vintage Books, 1961.

Watt, Ian. *The Rise of the Novel.* Berkeley and Los Angeles: University of California Press, 1965.

Weatherhead, A. Kingsley. *A Reading of Henry Green.* Seattle: University of Washington Press, 1961.

———. "Structure and Texture in Henry Green's Latest Novels." *Accent* 19 (Spring 1959):111–22.

Welty, Eudora. "Henry Green: A Novelist of the Imagination." *Texas Quarterly* 4 (1961):246–56.

Woolf, Virginia. *Granite and Rainbow.* New York: Harcourt, Brace and Co., 1958.

———. "Mr. Bennett and Mrs. Brown." In *Approaches to the Novel,* edited by Robert Scholes, pp. 187–206. San Francisco: Chandler Publishing Co., 1961.

Yeats, William Butler. *The Collected Poems.* New York: The Macmillan Co., 1962.

INDEX

TOWARD

LOVING

Composed in Linotype Caledonia with selected lines of display in Monotype Bulmer.

Printed letterpress on Warren's University Text, an acid-free paper watermarked for the University of South Carolina Press with the Press colophon.

Bound in Balacron 2200 series.

Composed, printed, and bound by Kingsport Press

Designed by Robert L. Nance